A Pint-sized History
of
Stoke-on-Trent
and District

Joan-Ann Grindley

Published by Sigma Leisure – an imprint of
Sigma Press, 1 South Oak Lane, Wilmslow, Cheshire SK9 6AR, England.

British Library Cataloguing in Publication Data
A CIP record for this book is available from the British Library.

ISBN: 1-85058-356-0

Typesetting and Design by: Sigma Press, Wilmslow, Cheshire.

Text and cover photographs: Chris Rushton

Printed by: Manchester Free Press

General Disclaimer

Whilst every effort has been made to ensure that the information given in this book is correct, neither the publisher nor the author accept any responsibility for any inaccuracy.

PREFACE

What is the connection between a quiet back-water village in Stoke-on-Trent and a saggar-walled dwelling where a young pottery genius hid from the evil eye of the local witch? What links the places where local delicacies have been devised and are still enjoyed, with freshly-mangled washing blowing in the yards of back-to-back houses?

The residents link all of these and many more communities in Stoke-on-Trent and its surrounding towns and villages. It is they who made this area their own.

But how can you learn about local history and traditions? There are precious few books and, over the years, many people have found that one of the best ways to learn about a community is by talking to its inhabitants – and by far the best place to find some of these wonderful local historians of Stoke-on-Trent is in a quiet corner of the nearest pub.

Like the variety of drinks that have always been supplied by local licensees over the years, the tales that the pottery people have to tell are numerous. Sometimes the stories are light and fanciful, with fairies and goblins abounding. Others, like strong beer, have fermented into a rich – if slightly heady – concoction of family deeds and church records.

Each one of the pubs mentioned in this volume has its own tale to tell which in itself could fill a book, but what has hopefully been achieved within these pages is simply a summary of how each area has developed: a potted, pint-sized history that should encourage readers to find out more for themselves.

The best way to enjoy this book is to leave it on the coffee table for a day or two. For although most books are meant to be read from beginning to end, this one is different. Take your cue from the illustration on the front cover: one of the best ways to relax is first to choose a good pub, then a drink that suits your individual taste, and savour them both before moving on.

Therefore, first choose a chapter of the book that tugs at your own heartstrings and then settle down for a good read. Once one chapter has been enjoyed, other parts of the book can slowly be consumed with relish.

After reading the parts that interest you the most, the next step is to spend a few minutes looking at the map, and then it's off to discover some interesting village or town for yourself. Don't worry if you have difficulty in finding the exact location mentioned – just pop into the nearest pub and ask for directions, but take care – each pub is full of its own 'pint sized history'.

Joan-Ann Grindley

Acknowledgements

I would like to thank all my friends who have helped with this book. Thanks in particular to: Gordon for his support and encouragement; Joy for the endless coffee; Jackie and John for their tireless endeavours to keep me and the text within the realms of reality; and Frank and the boys for their help and understanding. Also, a word of thanks to Fred Leigh for reading the book prior to publication and offering valuable information and comments.

This book is dedicated to my grandchildren.

Join Joan-Ann Grindley in . . .

Getting your bearings . . .

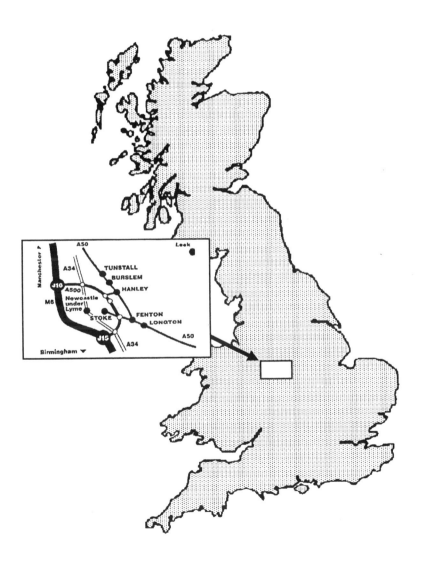

ABBEY HULTON

THE PRIORY

With street names such as Priory Road, Abbots Road and Friars Road the references to the former inhabitants of the area are all round the Priory Public House. Though the pub itself stands in Greasley Road it is difficult not to notice the history that is all around the area. But how did such a bleak area at the head of the River Trent become the place where the Cistercian monks chose to live? In fact, it was because of the clear River Trent and the streams that ran from the hills that the area was chosen.

It has been claimed that the river gained its name from the French connection that the area enjoyed over the years (*Trente* is French for thirty). At one time there were said to be thirty abbeys on its banks – but, as the river ran clear and fast long before the monks had discovered the fertile land of England, this is a dubious claim.

In 1200, Henry-de-Audley began the foundations for a monastery at an area we now call Carmountside, an area that was peaceful and safe from the heathens that still marauded the countryside. He dedicated the place to St. Mary.

The beautiful Abbey, which measured approximately 200 feet long and 100 feet across the transept, was dedicated in 1219 and its first Abbot was appropriately named Adam. The vows those monks obeyed were set down by St. Robert of Molesme, St. Aberic and St. Stephen Harding in 1098.

Those first monks wore white robes and followed a simple life of rising at 2 am to sing Divine Office. This was followed with prayer, meditation and the study of scriptures. Their main labour was on the land, producing the food they needed to survive, as well as wool from the flocks of sheep that were scattered on the wind-swept hillside. Under their supervision, small communities began to flourish. A mill was situated not far from the Abbey and people moved to the area, grinding corn for the monks who, in return, gave them the protection of their presence.

Milton was one of the many villages that grew at this time. The lands owned by the monasteries was immense, with parts of what is now Hanley and Bucknall all classed as part of their land. Some of the monastery land apparently extended as far south as Normacot, where 480 acres were owned and farmed by the monks. But, as with many estates, it is often quite difficult to identify the exact localities of the farms.

Much of the history of this time has been lost or destroyed over the years but from what has been recovered it seems that these people were not only farmers but also expert craftsmen, making pottery items. Fragments of these are among all that is left of the once-great monastery. Much of the area was vandalised – even the bones of some of the monks were dug up and scattered, so little regard did previous generations have for their heritage.

When Sir James Audley died, he left orders that he was to be buried before the high altar at his beloved Abbey at Hulton and £40 was to be distributed among the people to pray for his soul and £10 to be distributed to the monks of Hulton to remember him in their prayers. Twice-widowed Nicholas, fifth Lord of Audley, is said to be buried under the Choir of the Abbey Church along with his family; a stone coffin which now stands in St. Johns Churchyard, Burslem, is said to be that of one of his wives, Lady Elizabeth. This was possibly saved from scavengers.

It may also contain the remains of Sir Nicholas. Another curious twist in this tale is that in Buckfast Abbey, Devon, there is a tomb that bears the Audley coat of arms and it is claimed that this is the final resting place of not only James but also his brother Thomas. However, the genealogical table of the Audleys tells us that Thomas was fact buried in Audley Church.

The Dissolution of the Monasteries brought great changes to the countryside and, on the 18th September 1538, the Abbey at Hulton ceased to exist. So great was the land that the Church had owned in the Middle Ages that, before the dissolution, there were 77 Cistercian Abbeys in England. Most of the farming land of the Abbey was sold in 1545 to Edward Aston with Stephen Bagott buying the beautiful monastery bells.

Gradually, the land that was once so sacred to the people was left to the villagers. Perhaps it is fitting that the land that once echoed with the sounds of chants and prayers now rings out with the sounds of children's voices from the schools that are scattered around. Abbey Hill School is perhaps one of the best-known, catering for the needs of less-able children. Like the monks they to have rules to obey, like the monks they to have to learn that they are special people that may find it hard to adjust to the outside world, but with help they do.

Many people now live on the housing estate that makes up the community of Abbey Hulton and walk the streets that lead to and from the Abbey public house. The pub is still a popular meeting place, with an opportunity to enjoy the many different beers on offer. People often talk about the Abbey as though it was still a place of worship, with the bar as the high altar, but people in 500 years will be unlikely to talk of it with the same reverence as the first Abbey.

Only fragments remain of the great Abbey

ADDERLEY GREEN

THE CORNER PIN

Set in an area of less than six streets, the Corner Pin public house seems like just another pub in a suburb of Longton, with rows of houses all around and a few shops scattered about to attend to the needs of the inhabitants. This is where the similarity ends, as anyone who calls into the very solid-looking Corner Pin will find out. People born within the sights and sounds of Mossfield Colliery, locally called "The Old Sal Pit", share a deep affection brought about by generations of caring for each other in times of trouble, of which Adderley Green has had its share.

But how did the area that joins Bambury Street and Anchor Road become something to be proud of? When the pot banks of Longton and markets of Hanley were forming trading links with the industrial towns of the north, Adderley Green already had a heritage to call its own.

As the great Parish of Caverswall was beginning to grow, Saxon Chiefs were making small encampments around the surrounding countryside. The settlements of Werrington and Weston (Coyney) were slowly taking shape and secondary settlements were needed for the growing families. One Chief, Ealdred, chose a clearing in the woods to the west of Caverswall. He settled here, making rough shelters for himself and his followers, and guarding the area with a ferocity that gave him the reputation of a great warrior Chief.

Gradually, Ealdred's clearing or 'Lea' grew with the residents of the settlement. Although eager to forage the open fields of Berry Hill and the sand stone hills, collecting what they could to make their lives more comfortable, they were always thankful to come home to the comparative safety of the lush green Lea.

By the 1200s land ownership became an important part of life with the Aldthelegh family gaining and loosing areas frequently. Many savage fights took place, some might even have occurred over ownership of the land where the Corner Pin now stands. Perhaps this is where the caring nature of the people began, tending wounds and supplying drinks of nourishing ale to the weary.

The Subsidy Roll for 1327 not only shows the wealth of some of the people but also shows that the blood line of the Aderleys was still there, making the village very close-krit.

The pain and horror of the Black Death in the 1300s practically wiped out the village, nevertheless the Muster Roll of 1539 contains a Homfrey Adderley. Though not necessarily the same blood line, it proves that the community was beginning to grow again. A few families had survived, with new farmers taking advantage of the fertile soil around the land where the Stirrup and Pye pit was to be sunk later.

The Hearth Tax Returns of 1666 recorded the size of the settlements in the Parish and talks of a small settlement at Adderley. Because of the primitive nature of the dwellings, the number of family units is not recorded.

Gradually, pockets of cultivated areas began to spread out on the once completely open land around Longton. However the minerals that had lain dormant for centuries were slowly being discovered and smoke from the coal fires could be seen on the landscape.

When Dr Plott visited the area in the mid-1600s, on his journey to describe the features of England, he mentioned the coal exposures in the area. After conversations with William Parker, he discovered the dangers experienced by those people who tore coal from the earth to provide the fuel for the Pot Banks. What he did not mention was the deep companionship of the people who lived at Adderley that had built up after surviving the terrors of Highland Warriors marauding over their land and the Civil War with the Puritans' bleak rule.

Ward's directory of 1855 states little of the community that lived around Anchor Road, only that Geo. Forister was a farmer of some importance, Geo. Daniel a shopkeeper, Thomas Pye was a coal master, while Samuel Robinson owned licensed premises.

Coal mining was becoming an important part of the economy at this time. The sinking of so many pit shafts made any new building work in the area very hazardous, but still more shafts were sunk.

The rich Banbury and Cockshead seam of coal made the two shafts sunk by Messrs Hawley and Bridgewood in the mid-1800s quite profitable. The two cages were operated by one winding engine, with a three-shift system keeping the mine at Mossfield working all the time. The continuous sound of the winding gear becoming part of every day life, with people setting the time by the clattering of cloggs on the cobbled streets as the shift changed.

Every villager was connected in some way with the pit. Even the lines of washing hung out on Monday morning in yards around Stanfield

Street would somehow smell of the coal dust that filled the air. Small children used the slag heaps as playgrounds, the cables and trucks holding no fear to the innocent youngsters.

Life was hard within the community, sanitation was dismal with privies, ash pits and water taps shared by many families. The dust from the Old Sal and Sturrup and Pye pits covering everything and everyone.

Bathing, although looked on by many health experts at the time as a dangerous practice, was a necessity. Whatever the houses lacked, most had a tin bath that hung in the yard to be brought out, placed in the centre of the back-kitchen, and filled with the water heated up in the boiler in the corner. The smell of dinner cooking on the hob, the thought of a night out at the pub and maybe a song or two on the way home was something to look forward to.

Adderley Green land was cruel to its people though. The most dreaded sound in any mining village was that unmistakeable crack of an explosive blast, accompanied by the blaring colliery hooter, rousing the mining community from its sleep.

One such sound occurred on Wednesday October 16 1889 before the night shift had finished and the clock was yet to strike 4am. An explosion occured at the Mossfield Colliery, 'Old Sal'. The cry quickly spread through the streets. Wives and mothers scurried along Mossfield Road to the pit gates. The chaos that they found gave little comfort, and it was left to the old women of the village to give a small amount of hope to some and heartfelt condolences to others.

As the dawn light appeared over Park Hall hills the volunteers ventured into the dangerous ground below. A choking hell, reeking of coal and fumes. Men, boys and ponies were caught in that dreadful place. Gradually the rescuers discovered survivors, these were brought out, then the task that everyone hated, but at least it gave a little comfort to the bereaved families, the dead had to be brought out.

The lamp house became a mortuary, with the sobs of the otherwise silent crowd penetrating the cold morning air. Of the 80 workers that were trapped, only 13 survived, the rest including boys as young as 14 perished, with the bodies of 5 men never to be recovered. In nearby Longton Cemetery, a large inscribed cross marks the spot where 50 of the bodies were finally buried.

It took many years for the memory of that dreadful day to become less painful, but Adderley Green people have always had a strong respect for each other which carried on through the most troubled times, each person gaining strength from their friends and neighbours.

"In the midst of Life ✝ we are in Death."

In Memory of the

Sixty-Six Colliers

WHO LOST THEIR LIVES IN THE

Mossfield Colliery Explosion, Longton,

Wednesday, October 16th, 1889.

In perfect health they left their homes.
Not knowing that their time was come ;
A sudden change upon them fell,
No time to bid their friends farewell.

JACOB BATH, 33.
THOMAS BOUGH, 21,
THOMAS BRADSHAW.
WILLIAM BREWOOD, 29
JOHN BALL, 36
NOAH BALL, 41.
JOSEPH BULL, 58.
JOB BULL, 27.
JOSEPH BULL, 25.
WILLIAM BULL, 19.
JAMES BAILEY, 16.
THOMAS BROUGH.
JOHN BRADBURY
WILLIAM BURGESS, 40.
JOSEPH COTTON, 26.
HENRY CALCOTT, 25.
ISAAC DERRICOTT, 60.
ALBERT EDWARDS.
GEORGE EDWARDS. 42.
FRANK EMERY, 50.
WILLIAM FARRELL, 23.
JOSEPH EDWARDS. 57.

ARTHUR FLETCHER, 26.
FREDERICK HARES.
JONATHAN HARDING, 25
WM. HENRY HULME, 27.
DAVID HULME, 23.
DAVID HUGHES, 65.
WILLIAM HURST. 49.
JAMES HULSE, 26.
WM. B. HEATH. 34.
JOHN HALL, 16.
WM. JOHNSTONE, 34.
RICHARD JONES, 24.
JAMES B. JAMES, 23.
THOMAS JAMES, 18.
CHARLES JENKINS. 17
EDWARD JONES, 30.
WILLIAM LAWSON, 18.
JOHN MOORE, 31.
THOMAS MOFFATT.
EVAN PRICE, 27.
WILLIAM H. PLANT, 35.
SYDNEY RUTTER, 30.

GEORGE RATCLIFFE, 31.
WILLIAM SALTER, 48.
GEORGE STEELE, 14
JOHN STEELE, 16.
JOHN SMITH, 18.
WILLIAM SMITH, 16.
WILLIAM SIMPSON
GEORGE SALT, 42.
HERBERT SELLERS
JOHN SHENTON, 18.
THOMAS SHERWIN, 25.
SAMUEL SHERWIN, 18.
CHARLES SHERWIN, 21
FRANCIS M. SHAW. 26.
JOHN TOMLINSON, 32.
EDWARD TOWNSEND, 26.
THOMAS WALKER, 26.
SAMPSON WEDGWOOD 28.
SPENC'R WHITEHURST, 24
JOHN WILLIAMS, 17.
GEORGE WILSON.
HENRY WOOD, 20.

" WATCH : FOR IN SUCH AN HOUR AS YE THINK NOT THE SON OF MAN COMETH.'

The summer of 1902 brought great jubilation to the country, with Coronation celebrations taking place, all around Adderley Green, filling Bright Street and Weston Street with laughter as young and old alike made their way to the jollifications at Caverswall. The singing and dancing went on all day until the fading light drove the villagers home. The celebrations went on long into the night with the pub overflowing with people all sharing a glass or two of Joules ale.

The new generation of drinkers to the Corner Pin Public House has brought new problems and troubles to share, but one thing is certain: there are few problems that Adderley Green people have not had to face.

Just one more pub in a Longton suburb?

BIDDULPH

THE TALBOT

The cold winds from Mow Cop often blow icy blasts into the Talbot Inn at Biddulph, with regulars and visitors alike all wrapping up warm before going outside.

Nevertheless, local people are well-accustomed to the inhospitality of the bleak moorland and, with the help of their secret weapon, they can ward off colds and ills. The spring that bubbles to life on the hillside of Biddulph Moor has, so locals believe, medicinal qualities that will ensure good health to all that drink from it. The small trickle of water that first gives health to the people of Biddulph has, on its 170 mile journey to the North Sea, provided power to turn water wheels on its meanderings. Unfortunately, by the time it has reached Stoke, the River Trent has over the years become so polluted that, until quite recently, it was unfit to support life.

When the ancient Biddulph family built the Old Hall in approximately 1558 they thought the open position would help protect the family from trouble. Although the garrison stood firm, Cromwell's Army attacked relentlessly for three months and eventually most of the Hall was destroyed along with the small community. Even the beautiful church of St Lawrence suffered that dreadful summer. Only a few ornate monuments and the Flemish stained glass window of the church managed to be saved. It is hard to imagine what the community was like with frightened villagers hiding what they considered valuable from the marauding soldiers. With drinking and joviality banned, only the brave brewed the rough ale needed to sustain the soul.

Gradually, life became ordered again by the late 1600s with the open lands owned by the great families of the time. New words become absorbed into the language. The Old German word 'Dalrod' became fairly common to describe the Overlord or Commander of the Valleys, gradually becoming the family name of the Earls of Shrewsbury. Whether this is how their hunting dogs became known as Talbots or from the French nick-name 'Tailibe-bott' meaning gatherer of sticks can only be guessed at. Either way these sleek hunting dogs became a status symbol of the rich and were trained as carriage dogs. Although with selective breeding the large black and white dogs we now know as a

Dalmatian bears little resemblance to its ancient hunting forefathers the breed originates from. The name lives on to be given to the places where they were kept as pets or for work as carriage dogs. Although it is highly unlikely that the Talbot in Biddulph gained its name this way the heritage behind the name still gives the pub a special feeling.

By the early 1800s the small communities of Biddulph were growing with three silk mills providing work for the villagers. The water-powered mill at the Hurst appeared on a Tithe map dated 1840.

Major rebuilding was always taking place. The work done on the church was undertaken by T. Trubshaw and small schools were set up to educate the children.

The Grange became the focal point of the community with the turretted building surrounded by trees becoming the home of the great botanist James Bateman in the mid-1800s. The famous gardens, which were begun after the death of James' father, involved spectacular theme gardens that were to enthral the people then as now.

After the great fire, which destroyed the centre block of the Grange in 1896, it was left to Robert Heath to restore it to its former glory with the formal gardens and neatly-clipped hedges giving work to many local people.

By the 1900s the separate communities that made up what outsiders call Biddulph were growing. Each of the small villages developed their own personality. The Italianate Towers gave the Hurst area a romantic feel. Smoky chimneys of Black Bull and the wheels of Victoria Colliery at Brown Lees characterised the industrial parts of the area. The main village of Biddulph, with Barber's Picture Palace and its High street shops, began to encourage people to spend their hard-earned money.

Although busy trying to look forward after the horrors of the Great War, the people of Biddulph still found time to remember those who had died to make England a free land. Local stonemason Johan Cottrell created the granite memorial in the centre of the village, with its figure of a soldier which was unveiled in 1922.

The Heaths left the Grange in 1922. Transformation began to change what was a fine family house into a hospital, with the Prince of Wales officially opening the doors one rainy day in 1924.

Over the years many changes have taken place within Biddulph. Some older buildings have disappeared and others have had major face lifts. The renovations and opening of the beautiful Grange Gardens have brought new life into the area. The Talbot Inn now welcomes visitors who might not appreciate the outstanding beauty of the Rhododendrons and the delicate colours of the Camellias owes more than a little to the pure water of the area. The sparkle on the glasses and the healthy faces of the regulars around the bar in The Talbot shows that, although Biddulph has some heavy industry, the pure water and clear air will always help to keep its villagers in good health.

Biddulph Grange. "The majesty owes its existence to the trickle of water that starts in the hills"

BLURTON

THE SWALLOW'S NEST

Tucked away from the main road, the Swallow's Nest is one of those Public Houses that can easily be passed by. But like the area in which it is situated, once visited, it is never forgotten. Newstead, as it is known, has always been an interesting place with a history that goes back much further than the rows of trees that face the pub in Ufton Close.

Rows of trees still face the Swallow's nest

The estates of Trentham and Normacot stretched well beyond the present boundary of Waterside Drive in the time before the Domesday Book. Gradually groups of cottages began to take advantage of the hilly area which they called Blure, from the old word meaning a bubble or small swelling on the ground. Slowly a small town or village appeared in the meadow land.

By 1195 the village was called Bloreton. Other smaller communities gained their names many ways, some from the type of vegetation on the land – perhaps the Holly Bush gained its name this way. The Anglo-Saxon word *Hem* means 'border', therefore the Heath at the edge of Trentham easily became known as Hem Heath. And that small but delightful wooded area between Lightwood and Trentham just maybe gained its name from the old English word *Cocagne*, which translates to "A land of luxury and delight" whereas Newstead originally meant 'a recently marked position on the land'. This newly cultivated farming area was well known for the trees that marked out the meadow. Although *Blureton* (Blurton) is not mentioned in the Domesday Survey, like many other small communities it was included in one of the larger manors. Evidence of the community's existence is recorded in the Cartulary of Trentham Priory of 1348 which states that "John, son of Thomas-De-Blorton, exchanged six strips of land and a piece of meadow in a field called Fulfen and Bluremedewe." However, it does not state where the area of land lay.

At this time Trentham was the mother Church of the Parish although it is quite likely that a small Chapel existed at Blurton in 1400. Proof of this is on a Saxon map of 1577, where a small chapel of ease to Trentham Priory is marked.

The farms at Hem Heath and Penfold Farm supplied produce to be sold at the growing market towns of Hanley and Stone. These farms at Blurton straddled both sides of the main tracks and, as well as good arable land, they also used the readily available grazing land for sheep, fowl and cattle. Each farm supported the others in the village, especially in the autumn when groups of labourers moved from one farm to another, reaping, thrashing, bailing and gathering in the harvest to be stored in great barns for winter food. Thrashing was a long and tiring job that took place in the open fields between Blurton Priory and the Chapel. An Old English word for this procedure was 'drubbing', and perhaps the lane that joins Trentham Road to Church Road gained its name from the land where many hours of this work took place. Although the maps of the late 1800s show no such place as Drubbery Lane, a field is marked as Blubber Lea. Perhaps the name grew from the spring that bubbled into the fresh water well in Church Lane by Stanley's Cottage, or is a derivation of the word drubbery. Either way parts of the lane contain some of the oldest cottages in the area.

Other trades were beginning to set up at this time, providing work for the people of Blurton. The Shelters that provided a safe refuge for the villagers were made from local material. The marshy land that ran beside Blurton Brook provided the reeds to make the warm thatch for the roofs. The men who worked the thatch were very experienced in their trade using the needles, eaves knifes and combed legged tools, both skilfully and quickly ensuring each home was prepared for the long cold winters.

By the time the Meir to Trentham road was turnpiked at Hem Heath in the 1700s, the township of Blurton was flourishing. The outlying farms at the Grange and Crowcroft employed many casual labourers who had begun to move out of the ever-growing towns. The 314 acres farmed to Newstead was perhaps the largest of these, with many labourers living-in during the summer.

Gradually, industry was creeping into the area in the early 1900s, with the two tileries supplying the red bricks and slates needed in such quantity for the new buildings that were springing up. The only evidence left of their existence is perhaps Tillery Road and memories of clay items that were once manufactured at Copshurst, an area between Lightwood and Cocknage.

Good housing was becoming a priority by the 1900s and gradually the view from the small bell tower of Blurton Chapel was changing, with new houses filling the once open fields. After World War II, the great farming estates were beginning to disappear, making way for rows of houses that linked Windborne Road and Waterside Drive with Barlaston Road. This created the small village of Newstead with schools, churches and shops all on hand to provide the inhabitants with modern-day amenities.

In 1924, the fifth Duke of Sutherland had the first spade of soil dug out for Hem Heath Colliery and the industrialisation of Blurton had begun. Although the winding-gear, machinery and slag-heaps had altered the view from the main road, the hilly land that first gave the ground its name protects the area around the Swallows Nest from the busy industry. The pub stands proudly in Newstead with all the facilities of a modern drinking place, a dance floor and music to suit all tastes. Good food and drink all encourage people to make the Swallows Nest a great place to have a celebration drink or a quiet night out with a few friends.

BLYTHE BRIDGE

THE SMITHFIELD HOTEL

With its proximity to the railway line and the busy A521, it is easy to see why the Smithfield Hotel is always busy. But people don't always use the long rooms for a quick drink; many plan an evening's celebration within the friendly rooms. The spotlessly clean, richly-carpeted floors and soft music are very different from the Smithfield where many men met in the early 1900s. In times gone by, as soon as the piercing sound of the Station master's whistle at the Station across the road was heard, men and boys would scramble out of the tiny front door of the Smithfield to join the throngs of people clambering for a better view of the cattle for sale. A builder's merchants now occupies the building that was once filled with the sights and sounds of a busy cattle market.

Blythe Bridge has much more than the remains of a station to offer, as any regular who stands at the bar of the pub will tell you.

With a gentle river to support life and give pleasure, it did not take long for a settlement to grow. First, the settlers forded the river, then they built a small wooden bridge across the main track to Uttoxeter.

The community of Blythe Bridge grew with the level ground before the crossing and the marshy ground beyond all using the main village as a meeting place. By the mid-1700s, the £37 left in a Charity Trust by William Amery provided a tiny school which had been demolished by 1879, to be replaced by a Grand Hall known by all as Blythe Bridge House. The hall which was situated on high ground faced the tiny row of houses in Church Terrace. All that is left of the house, whose occupants included T.C. Wild and Charles Harvey, are a few bricks scattered around the retaining walls of the main road, and perhaps a gate post or two to show where it once stood.

By the mid-1800s, the great railway companies were beginning to form a network of lines across the area and, on the 7th August 1848, Blythe Bridge Station was opened to the public. Frock-coated William Vyse, the Station Master, welcomed people with a tip of his hat on that day and for many years to come. Modern technology came slowly to Blythe Bridge and the tiny Rose Cottage dealt with the few phone calls that the important people of the village had until recent years.

To most people, the only form of transport was the pony and trap that was looked after with great care by the local blacksmith. Nevertheless, the motor car did come to the area and, by the turn of the century, the Smithfield Hotel was offering refreshment to "Refined Travelling Gentlemen" on their way to the larger towns and cites. The quarried floored bar also became a meeting place for the local farm workers.

Gradually, public transport became an important part of village life with the proprietor of the Smithfield, Arthur Keeling, in 1921 starting a bus service from Cheadle to Longton using the Smithfield as its depot. The service became known as the "Old Bill." Journeys on the bus took quite a time with frequent stops for overheated engines and livestock on the road, as well as the bus driver having to help the passengers on and off. Although hazardous, the friendly drivers took great pride in their buses, with quite a few hours spent cleaning them in the yard of the Smithfield Hotel.

Of the many people that were seen travelling past the Smithfield between the wars, perhaps the most memorable was Mr. Meigh. He was said to keep his money under the hat that he always wore, and would

In this building, the "Old Bill" started

willingly give a short ride in his opened topped sports car to anyone, but as the sign said on the side "at the passenger's own risk." There was also Mrs. Mulinner and her bicycle with a box on the front containing delicious ice cream that she would sell at the road side, and the old bearded postman who travelled the lanes, delivering the post as well as spreading the local news; the list is endless.

The Smithfield, or as it is now affectionately called "The Smithy", has undergone many structural changes over the years and Blythe Bridge Station exists no more. What is left remains as a permanent memorial to those who have gone before. Hopefully with the major A50 taking traffic away from the village, Blythe Bridge and the Smithfield can keep the fragments of its history that has been left.

Blythe Bridge station, 1950

BUCKNALL

THE TRAVELLER'S REST

People have for many years enjoyed the hospitality of the Travellers Rest, in Bucknall, with each of its rooms having a personality of its own. From the serenity of the Chapel of Rest to a busy entertainment area, all are connected by a welcoming bar that greets the passing visitors as they walk through traditional swing doors facing the busy main Werrington Road. The other doors equally welcoming, making a quick way in for the regulars as they walk along the suburban Ruxley Road. For many years this has made the Travellers Rest the place to go in Bucknall for a good night out.

Even though the pub itself has had a chequered history, of which each of the older residents is only too eager to give his version, the small community of Bucknall has always managed to keep some of the secrets of its past well-hidden.

Although the area between Werrington Road and Dividy Road has changed little since the turn of the century with streets of neat houses, each row with a shop, business or public house on the corner, it has always given the appearance of a special place.

The residents of the area that borders the main Leek Road and Townsend have maintained the continuity of their community life for many years but will always help the passing stranger. With good farming land and quick-witted people, the community has asked for very little from the rest of the district. Perhaps the original settlers left more than the name as a legacy of their presence.

The name itself probably originates from one of the invading warriors who were colonising many parts of Britain in approximately 400 AD. A fierce chief by the name of Bucca found a secret place hidden from the marauding Celts sheltered by the moorland and hills to the south and west and the wooded area to the north and east. Here, he decided to make a stockade for his small band of followers not far from the fast-flowing River Trent, between the two fresh water brooks alive with fish to provide an easy supply of food for his companions.

Gradually Bucca's secret place grew but with scrubland all around its secrets were well kept. Slowly war-like warriors turned into the first farmers of England. They tended the fertile land around the Eaves area, building shelters for themselves and their beasts on the high ground and strip-cultivating the fields, which was a fair way of ensuring every man had some good land to provide corn to feed his family and barley to make the ale so important to quench their thirst.

Other settlements began to grow with a simple form of bartering and trading beginning. A primitive trading road appeared between *Chedle* (Cheadle) and *Hanley Green* (Hanley) which soon became busy with pack-horses, cattle and carts, this made the tracks like a stagnant swamp in the winter and caked rock hard in the summer. Wheels soon became buckled and broken with the tired travellers needing a place to rest and enjoy some fresh food.

First, the scattered dwellings along Werrington Road bartered for what they needed, like pots and pans for the home-brewed ale, bread and freshly-slaughtered meat. The populace then began to specialise to supplement meagre finances. Ale houses, bakeries and slaughter houses began to attend to the needs of newcomers and villagers alike, as well as ostlers to tend to the horses and wheelwrights to repair the broken carts.

An important commodity of these people was wood, so readily available from the densely wooded area towards Wetley Moor. Many of the trees that helped to keep the settlements secret were felled, with great logs lying in piles and pits around the Fellbrook and Birch Gate areas. Rough Shelters began to form into a village of thatched cottages all huddled together to protect them from the wild animals that still abounds in the area.

The main wood trade was in the giant oak, which supplied beams for landowners' and villagers' homes, bark for tanning, acorns to feed the pigs, and even galls as a dye. Other trees were also used. Beech, with its close grain, was ideal for butter casks, while the flexibility of the willow made the milkmaids' yokes easier to carry; alder with its lightness made excellent clogs and the sturdy elm was ideal for coffins. Often, the struts of the carts to carry these goods were made of ash, its elasticity giving it many uses.

Smaller trades set up in the yards behind the cottages around the Malthouse area, too far from the main road to attract the passing trade but quiet enough for the delicate art of whittling and turning. These craftsmen made beautiful walking sticks, carved furniture and elegant tankards, to be used at grand banquets and ale houses alike.

Many of these early village trades have completely disappeared from the Bucknall of today but maybe some of the modern traders can, with a little imagination trace their beginnings back to this time.

By the 1600s, village life had settled into a steady pace, with traders and villagers all enjoying the hospitality of the ale house which served a rough brew from locally-grown barley and malt stored in buildings around the area where the Mary Bourne Home now stands.

However, with prosperity came disease. Rats were brought into buildings tucked into bundles of clothes purchased from pedlars. Villagers grew to disregard their presence, and only when tales of a dreadful pestilence were brought into the ale house by travellers on their way from London to the North did the village elders begin to worry, but by then it was too late: the Black Death had come to Bucknall.

At first, the naive country-dwellers believed it was a punishment from God and they spent many hours praying for forgiveness in the beautiful Church of St Mary. Only when they realised that both old and young, rich and poor were affected did they try to stop its spread, but without the knowledge of hygiene the small community was practically wiped out. Grave diggers worked feverishly until they too were struck down and still the numbers increased. With crops left to rot in the field around the Ruxley Road area the farms at the crossing fell into disrepair and few people ventured beyond their own homes. Ale houses stood empty as the plague took its toll and the village slowly ground to a halt.

Time passed and the village slowly recovered. The few farmers that had survived began to tend the fields that had lain fallow. They took produce along the Bucknall Road to Hanley Green in exchange for nails and clothes, and along the Werrington Road for livestock and to hire workers from the annual market at the as yet-unnamed Cellarhead. Bucknall people were still regarded as part of a close-knit community and they, in turn, had little time for the rougher townspeople.

The peace again was shattered in 1745 when marauding Highland warriors were marching across the area. Frightened villagers kept indoors and windows were bolted, food and ale well-hidden underground and the simple foundries worked hard to produce locks and bolts. The sudden warning cries of the animals in their pens brought fear into their hearts.

Eventually, fear turned to complacency and village life returned to a pleasant scene again, with some of the most popular pastimes being dancing and beer drinking. Bucknall villagers grew in health and prosperity.

The turnpiking of many main tracks in 1764 improved slightly the dreaded journey over water-logged ground. Many of the village traders feared that the general improvement in road conditions would mean that passers-by would not pause at Bucknall, but they adapted well and people carried on using the trades on offer.

Into this idyllic life came a new fear. On cold winter's nights, beer was consumed not only for pleasure but to give courage to the travellers as they journeyed along the lanes, with goods bought and sold. Thieves, highwaymen, witches and evil spirits abounded at the beginning of the 1800s along Werrington Road. A tale is still told today of one young man who was known as Sauntering Ned who travelled the lanes from Hanley to Cheadle with pots to sell and food to buy. The road through Bucknall was particularly hazardous, with thick bushes and dark corners. He took the trouble of protecting himself by attaching horns and bells to his pack animal, giving the appearance of the dreaded devil. This worked well – so well that one evening, while he was passing St Marys churchyard, he came across grave robbers going about their evil trade. On hearing the bells and seeing the horns, the villains took fright, leaving behind their horse and cart. Our hero attached his pack animal to the cart and carried on to Cheadle. As no one claimed them, he kept them and from then on, the young man's fortunes increased and he became a well-known haulage contractor.

John Wesley's Methodism came to Bucknall in the mid 1800s, with quite a few of the residents still today enjoying his form of Christianity at the simple little chapel in Chapel Street.

When the 1900s dawned so did that dreadful world war, taking many of the young men away from their families to fight in far-off places like Guise and Marne. Very few of the straw-boatered young men returned home and those who did were always to be haunted by the ones they left behind. Everything had changed in those dreadful four years, but with good friends spending time with the war veterans and maybe sharing a gill or two in drinking houses like the Travellers Rest they were able to talk of their ordeal with other ex-service men and to stand proud on Remembrance Sunday at the Cenotaph in the cemetery.

As the years passed, the people and traders that first breathed life into Bucknall have altered with wheelwrights changing to garages, and carters to haulage contractors. Slaughter houses, bakeries, clog makers and houses where home-cooked food could be bought have changed to shoe shops, butchers, grocers, bakers and the ever-popular fish and chips shop. The once-busy coffin makers have become discreet undertakers and ale houses that were once in the front rooms of farms have become grand public bars.

The visitors have changed too – from travellers on horseback on their way to the market towns, to customers arriving in their cars or on the buses that run a frequent service along the ancient trading tracks.

Although this history has mentioned few of the personal details of the people of Bucknall, this is how it should be: leaving some secrets to the inhabitants and regulars who just might share a tale *Regulars in the Chapel of Rest might share a tale or two* or two with the visitors to the Travellers Rest.

BURSLEM

THE GEORGE

Standing proudly at the corner of Swan Square and Nile Street, the George Hotel overlooks the town. People go about their daily tasks, barely pausing to glance up at the majestic building that has given a welcome to visitors for more years than anyone can remember. With its grand rooms, magnificent bars and fine stables the George Hotel has always been the place to visit for refreshments, to meet with friends and to talk.

On a cold winter's night, conversation might turn away from the football match at nearby Port Vale ground or the latest production at the Queens Theatre, to a time when Burslem was little more than a village. It had cottages with broken saggars for walls, clods for roofs and people coming from far away to see "The Big House" that the Wedgwood family had built in 1751. However, the history of Burslem goes much further back than that.

The Domesday Book records Burslem (*Barcardeslim*, also known as *Burwardeslym*, or *Borewareslam*, derived from the Saxon *Bur* = retired dwelling, *wardes* = towards, and *lime* = woodland tract) as a "solitary dwelling near a wood". Few serfs lived there, and those that did only just managed to eke out a meagre existence on the land that was wet, clayey and in most parts unsuitable for cultivation. Gradually man's need for personal property grew and those who lived by the yet-unsullied streams began to use the only asset they had. The clayey soil, so difficult to cultivate, was dug out to leave marl holes. Lean-to extensions with a simple throwing area were added to their homes and pots were made, first for the family's own use, then to supplement their meagre finances. Bartering took place, and traders came along the lanes, past the Saxon Church of St John, to the market-place. Goods were exchanged for pottery, which was sold as they travelled north to Congleton and beyond. With this simple beginning the Mother Town of the pottery industry was born. As Doctor Plott recorded at the end of the 17th century, Burslem was the greatest seat of the Pottery industry in Staffordshire.

The late 1600s brought great changes to Burslem. Fresh water was scarce and the drinking of cheap ale was one of the main pastimes of the people around St John's Square, Greenhead and Swan Square.

With inadequate food and bad living conditions many people had some kind of deformity. These people were looked on as evil and many tales were spread about them. Innocent tales would get exaggerated, possibly because of the ale drunk, and witch hunting had swelled to a frenzied fever by the turn of the 1700s.

Villagers of Swan Bank area began gathering in corners of the ale houses to talk of the strange woman who would not attend the newly-extended St John's Church and lived at the cottage at Hamil with hawthorn bushes that never blossomed and a black raven as a pet. Was it true that her evil eye could turn milk sour before it left the cow? Could a word from her have caused the dreaded smallpox that left Josiah Wedgwood weak and caused his right leg never to recover?

When poor Molly Leigh died in 1748, no one shed a tear. In an attempt to pacify her soul, she was buried in the reverse of the customary orientation: south to north. After the simple funeral at St John's Church, Parson Spencer first led the party of mourners past Birch Croft to a local hostelry to gain sustenance and then onwards to the cottage. Parson Spencer hesitated on the threshold of the cottage. Whether it was his imagination or the wines and spirits he had imbibed, but there sitting by the fireside was Molly, and on her shoulder sat her pet blackbird. The parson with his cronies in tow, ran back to the town as fast as their legs could carry him.

The story goes that four members of the clergy at the stroke of midnight, clad in vestments and chanting prayers, walked full of apprehension into the churchyard. The sexton and clerk walked in front carrying spades and lanterns and, without further ado, started to re-open the grave. Soon, there was the soft thud of spade against coffin. Somewhere in the night, a blackbird croaked. Three of the clergymen fled in terror, but Parson Spencer was resolved to lay the ghost of Molly once and for all. Lifting the lid of the coffin and, by the dim light of the lantern, he once again saw the body of Molly. Was that a wry smile on her face? He hurriedly laid the pet raven by her side and closed the lid.

The parson then proceeded to the cottage, and there said prayers that the ghost would not trouble them any more.

Is Molly finally at rest?

As the 1700s wore on, so did the need for a better life for the people of England. In 1760, John Wesley and a companion entered Burslem on horseback; they rode from Pack Horse Lane into the open space at St John's Square to preach. Most of the assembled people stood in quiet admiration, but a few hooligans pelted him with clods and eggs. However, these few did not deter him and he often returned to Burslem, preaching to ever larger crowds and sometimes to visit his old friends, the Bourne family. Throughout his life John Wesley was to mention how devout the people of Burslem had become.

July 26, 1766, was a great day in the life of the people of Burslem. A general holiday was declared and people from neighbouring towns poured into the Dale Hall area. In the centre stood Josiah Wedgwood and James Brindley. After the formal speeches, James Brindley dug out the first spade of turf that heralded the beginning of the Grand Trunk Canal. After the Good Health of all concerned was toasted from a barrel of fine ale, everyone adjourned to their favourite hostelry for banquets. Never before had Burslem seen such rejoicing.

Life settled into a steady pace by the beginning of the 1800s, with the town growing rapidly. Then, came the Battle of Waterloo.

Many of the young men went away to fight, leaving behind a quiet town. On their return Burslem became busy again with gifts and souvenirs for everyone. Swan Square became the place to be seen, the George Hotel busy with soldiers, each telling their own tale punctuated with mementoes. Among these were many horse shoes and nails picked up from the battle ground; many are said to be buried outside the George Hotel under that fine road that was to be finished only two years after the battle. Waterloo Road will always be a great reminder of those days.

1842 brought the Chartist Riots to Staffordshire. With the George Hotel standing as it does on the main road from Hanley to the south, it saw many battles outside its grand facade. In the summer of that year, the Chartist marchers entered the doors and caused a great deal of damage to the interior. One protagonist, known locally as Cogsey Nelly, stood fast as the soldiers advanced into the now-devastated rooms that were once pleasant bars. But the poor hungry collier was soon over-powered and finally evicted from the premises.

Then the dreaded Riot Act was read out in Swan Square and the Battle of Burslem began. Muskets rang out and frightened townspeople hid in the beer cellars of the public houses until the militia cleared the town of rioters. Many died in the ensuing battle that dreadful summer. Records show that one young man met his sad death outside the iron gates of the Red Lion; he is buried at his home town of Leek with the epitaph "I went up to town a sight to see and met a shot that killed me." Among those who did survive the battle was Cogsey Nelly who, after a trial and spell in solitary confinement, was deported to the colonies.

By the start of 1900, Burslem's fortunes were growing, with major factories carrying out their trade from imposing buildings throughout Burslem. Thos Hughes' factory at Swan Square and the glass works below employed many people, several of whom would probably spend some of their spare time frequenting the George Hotel. The factory management using the well lit rooms and drinking fine beer. While the workers choose the sawdust floored bars, drinking rough ale and being entertained by singers with popular songs of the day.

The hard work and living conditions made the need for relaxation a necessity. While most of the men enjoyed the hospitality of the George

Hotel and maybe a game of billiards. The more genteel of the townsfolk observed religious events.

One that was celebrated throughout Burslem around the area where the Maypole once stood, near to the Methodist Church, Wedgwood Place was "Lifting" on Easter Monday to celebrate the "Raising of the Lord." It was the practice to place a person in a chair and lift them as high as possible three times. After donations were collected, a social tea and simple party were held. However, with the increase of a rougher element in the area around Hamil Road this practice was first ridiculed and then abandoned.

Arnold Bennett wrote eloquently about Burslem in the latter part of the 19th century and the early part of the 20th, changing *The George* to *The Dragon* in his book "Clayhanger". Much has changed, but hopefully Burslem will always remain in the hearts of everyone as the Mother Town of the Potteries.

BUTT LANE

THE MILLSTONE

Like looking at snap shots of the past, Butt Lane evokes memories of a time when people enjoyed the simple things in life, as well as taking great pride in their surroundings. Perhaps the Millstone Public House Butt Lane is the nearest that people of today can get to this. Clear cool beer is served in dimpled glass mugs, almost exactly as it has been for more years than people can remember.

Passing the time of day before beginning the housework

To those who live beyond the two crossroads that enclose the area, Butt Lane means very little. Its greatest claim to fame is that 115, Congleton Road was the birth place of Reginald Mitchell – the designer of the Spitfire aeroplane. In most history books it states that he was born in a small area near Talke. Older members of this close-knit community are horrified when people say, "Butt Lane, where's that?"

The area around the Millstone is full of history and until the road planners decide that the area would make a "super slip road for the M6" it can remain intact, even if shorn of a few of its landmarks.

Perhaps the heyday of Butt Lane was the early 1900s when the area, like many others, had a grand community spirit. Rows of neat houses backed on to each other and faced the main roads, many with just a door and step or two to separate home from the outside world. A world full of coal dust and dirt from the nearby pits.

Armed with pail and step stone, shawled and white-aproned ladies could be seen most days in Skellen Street occasionally passing the time of day with neighbours as they whitened their steps. Even the slightly grander bay-fronted houses in Congleton Road had porches to cardinal red and window ledges to be wiped down; only heavy rain called a halt to this weekly ritual.

Later in the day, these same ladies could be seen walking along Woodshutt Street to one of the many corner shops in Chapel Street. This was not only for food and cleaning materials: occasionally, enough money was left to buy a hank or two of wool, with the rest 'laid by', to knit a pullover for the head of the house.

Much enjoyment was gained from this simple hobby which often, on summer evenings, took place while sitting outside the front door of the houses in Skellen Street.

But nothing compared with the thrill of seeing the 'Perils of Pauline' on the silver screen at the cinema which stood next to the old wooden smithy, just over the road from Butt Lane Co-op. A night out at the Picture Palace would, more often than not, end with just enough time to call in the local for a pint of Mackeson before heading along Woodshutt Street and home.

Many of these simple pleasures could have ended with the great depression of the 1920s which brought hardship to everyone. Butt Lane people had to find ways of making sure that there was enough money left at the end of the week for a pint. With no spare pennies after the tally-man and the rent man had called new clothes were a luxury few could afford. Worn out pullovers became socks, shawls and even small trousers after first going through the process of unpicking then being wound into skeins, washed gently in the tin bath and allowed to dry on the back of a chair. After this came the arduous task of winding the wool into balls, which often involved small fidgety children. But this was not the only way of making new from old. Worn out shirts became aprons, sheets which had already been patched became bolster cases and even rags were used to make sturdy rugs. Not even buttons were discarded – they were put into the button box to be used later.

Gradually, a little prosperity came back to the area, with the customers of Stevenson's shop at the corner of Congleton road finding enough money for sugared almonds as a treat.

Perhaps many think of Butt Lane people as being trapped in a time-warp of poverty. But, like most small villages, old traditions die hard and many older people are still noted for their ways of making money spin out. To outsiders, the hard times are like a millstone to be carried about. Many people think that the pub has a name that is very apt, but the customers of today only occasionally talk of the past. More often, regulars at the Millstone Public House talk of hope for the future and of the simple pleasures we would all like to enjoy.

CAVERSWALL

THE AUCTIONEERS ARMS

To most people the fact that the tiny village of Caverswall has a castle is just part of everyday life with the gate house and towers barely noticeable. Although many histories have been compiled about Caverswall, the tales all seem to centre around the square and the rich people of the manor, of days before the Constable-wick tree and the village stocks caused problems to the motor cars. The outskirts of the village have just as important a part in the village history, with the area around the "Knock-em-down", Cookshill, as people from miles around call the Auctioneers Arms, filled with as many tales as the Square.

The village church of St Peter's was consecrated in 1230. Records state that a moated castle was standing on the site of the present castle by 1322. With the farmland to the west of the village becoming known as the place where the best food was produced.

Originally the green where the Auctioneers Arms now stands was just that, a piece of green land where people met, cattle were bought and sold and animals grazed.

The farms that shaped Caverswall began to grow by the 1600s with layered hawthorn hedges separating the land, and clear brooks with fast flowing tributaries cutting through the fields and tracks. This water was, at first, forded in places; then, small bridges appeared to help people stay drier when driving the cattle home. One perfect example of this is the tiny foot-bridge known to most people as part of their childhood memories as the bridge at Mill Brook.

Gradually, firmer bridges were built for the heavier carts needed to supply the village with goods it could not produce itself. Although the road has been improved many times over the years, the arch and blocks that the first builder used can still be seen on the underside of the bridge that crosses the brook on Caverswall Road near the Cricket Club.

World events, although dramatic at the time, made little difference to the general growth of the village. By the mid-1800s, affluent people and squires had begun to build short rows of cottages for the workers at the edge of the main village. Although many of these houses had only tiny gardens, the farm labourer never went without fresh food as many were paid in produce as well as a meagre wage.

The area around the Auctioneers Arms became popular. As well as having a pub which supplied the best ale for miles around, it was a good meeting place – being at the junction where the small communities of Weston Coyney, Roughcote and Sheepwash met. The families of Caverswall were poor in comparison with families of the growing towns of Meir and Longton. What village people had were the fields, lanes and woods supplying endless fresh food for free.

Nevertheless even in the enlightened time between the wars many adults of the village were nervous about the woods and many believed in evil spirits. The sermons preached from the pulpit in St Peters Church, with the beautiful organ built by Oaks of Meir Heath as a memorial to the Glorious Dead, fell on deaf ears when strange happenings occurred in the Church grounds. Only innocent young children knew the truth: the only fairies and goblins that lived in Caverswall then were good ones. The evil ones had been banished by the Reverend Macnamara as he travelled the lanes in his open top carriage, or changed into Gargoyles that still peer accusingly from the Church.

Surely only good fairies could have made such beautiful rings at Cookshill. Why else would groups of acorn shells have been found close by, if it was not that a fairy ball had been held on a moonlit night? And if, after careful investigation, a secret pathway was discovered deep in Hardiwick Wood only the rough boys saw it as a rabbit path; little girls knew the truth, eagerly gathering the delicate flower petals that had fallen from tiny dresses as the little people had made a quick get-a-way.

Warm summer days brought the girls and boys out to play, skipping along the lane past the Auctioneers Arms along by the edge of the brook until Nunns Bridge came into sight. Although not particularly interesting to adults every child knew the sheer thrill of building a dam with clods and stones gathered from the surrounding area. As the water rose so did the living creatures, all eagerly caught in nets and jars. Boys caught only small silver fishes called by everyone "Bully Heads". While girls searched for mermaids and frogs that had once been princes and princesses.

Can 'Bully Heads' still be caught in Mill Brook?

Gradually these small children grew but they still loved the area between Yew Tree Farm and Vicarage Farm. As the summer sun began to ripen the corn so the lanes and hedgerows turned a rosy hue with enough fruit to supply the villagers throughout the year.

The gathering of nature's harvest was quite an event in village life. The first soft fruits were ready for picking in late June, with whole families taking large baskets. These might contain sandwiches of last year's jam and a bottle of water or perhaps a bottle of pop secured with a glass stopper and wire. They would walk along Roughcote Lane to Caverswall Common to find a suitable area where the trees were easy to reach. Gradually the heavily-laden baskets were set down and the simple picnic was consumed. Only when the evening light faded did the family head home with jams to make. Later the blackberries and bilberries were ready to turn fingers and hands blue-black. The heavy work of apple gathering was left until after the corn had been harvested, with the men being encouraged to help with the promise of a glass or two of home-made wine. This wine compared favourably with anything the licensee of the local pub would sell and was made from a great variety of ingredients. One local favourite was Elderflower Champagne with its rich flowery taste and after a while on the stillage in the cottages was consumed with great care.

Although many fields around the Auctioneers Arms have been replaced with the modern houses of Holyhead Crescent and York Road, just here and there remnants of long summer days remain. Stepping stones in Mill Brook, straw piled high in the hay loft at Greens Farm and sheep and cattle grazing in fields around the Auctioneers Arms.

Perhaps one day, the few people who are left, will tell their grandchildren stories of Blackberry Jam and "Bully Heads", of evil goblins turned into stone, and rocks on street corners that still bear a resemblance to Dragon eggs. All these things and many more have been left by generations that have all loved the area around the Auctioneers Arms.

CELLARHEAD

THE HOPE AND ANCHOR

A public house has stood at this site for over 150 years, although strong ale has been drunk here for many years.

In the early 16th century, the main living was on the land with peasant farmers settling down to a jug of ale after tending their livestock on the flat ground towards Wetley Moor.

In late 1745, Bonny Prince Charlie's army marched in disarray from Leek towards Derby, passing the few dwellings that stood bleakly against the sky-line. It is likely that more than a few gills of ale were consumed to ward off those cold north winds.

By the 1750s, a slender network of cottage industries had begun to alter the landscape. The nailmakers at Cellarhead made a dramatic change to the once peaceful surroundings with a smell and noise that filled the air. These labourers would have quenched their thirst here after the hard daily toil

Just before Christmas of that year came the cattle plague that depleted the small cattle farms. The smell of burning carcasses made drink a necessity. By 1764, Cellarhead had three turnpike roads (but alas no name) and a few scattered settlements now recovered from that dreadful plague.

Sometime after the American War of Independence in 1776, the "volunteers" returned home to much jubilation and merry-making, with wounds to heal and gifts to share. The cotton plant that flourishes on Wetley Moor is said to have been brought back by the men.

Trading links had been formed by 1825 between the industrial towns and farming settlements with weekly market days and the two great fairs on May 5th and November 5th. This was when modern Cellarhead was born.

The tents and gaudy caravans filled the field between what is now the chapel and the Hope and Anchor. Bare-fist fighting, bull-baiting and all the other gory entertainments then popular were staged not only on the great fair days but throughout the year. With the traders shouting their wares, one voice stood out from the crowd, that of a swarthy gypsy, who set up her tent selling ale and various items she had gathered on her journeys round the villages. Gradually, her reputation began to grow and her selling prose spread by word of mouth along the lines of "That Gypsy will sell-y-ed". After a time, to go to see "Sell-y-ed". meant to go to the fair.

By 1851, the ale tent had been replaced by stone block buildings with a Methodist chapel being built sometime later on the spot where once bulls were baited to a cheering crowd. Cellarhead had now come of age.

Of the four pubs that once stood at the crossroads, only the Hope and Anchor still remains. The Spotted Cow was replaced by the bowling green and the other two have gone forever.

Whites directory of 1851 reported one of the leading citizens as Thomas Heath of the Hope and Anchor. Over the years, with alteration and rebuilding, the premises have changed but there are still many traces of that inn that once gave shelter and refreshment to the travelling characters that lived here before the motor car.

Cellarhead, where once the bulls were baited

DILHORNE

THE ROYAL OAK

Like the great tree, The Royal Oak stands majestically in the centre of Dilhorne. The occasional horse-drawn vehicle seems somehow less out of place than the passing motor car that sometimes is lucky enough to discover the little village. Driving around the New Road corner, it is tempting to stop at The Royal Oak with its neat windows, fine beer and doors that seem to call out a welcome to everyone who passes.

Most people stop at the Royal Oak!

However, don't be misled into thinking the 20th century has passed Dilhorne by. Most older residents know that some families like to live in busy towns and cities, with hypermarkets and take-aways close by, but Dilhorne people have chosen to live in a village that has tried to keep the heritage that was bestowed on them long ago.

Marauding warriors from France had begun to colonise many parts of Britain in approximately 400 AD. But the hilly land between the *Fotes* (Forsbrook) and *Werringas* (Werrington) settlements proved inhospitable, with foxes and wolves still abounding in the woods and thickets. Each of the warrior chiefs fiercely guarded his settlement, knowing little of the existence of other encampments beyond the horizon, living what was a very singular and bleak life.

When their families grew, secondary settlements appeared, Roughcote and Brookhouses began to afford shelter for the young warriors' families. Gradually they began to grow braver and ventured beyond the comparative safety of their own encampments to discover new areas to cultivate. At first they thought the land between Hardiwick and the Callow Hills was uninhabitable, but then they discovered rich mineral deposits and this area became known as *Dulver* from the Anglo-Saxon word *Delve* or Dig.

The simple farmers at the time of the Domesday survey had begun to make *Dulva* (Dilhorne) a thriving but sparsely populated settlement, with strips of land being cultivated between the hills and woods that covered the Caverswall and Kingsley Moor area.

By the time the All Saints Church was consecrated in 1166, the villagers not only lived in fear of the wrath of God, but also the anger of the Lord of the Manor who dealt out punishments for the law breakers. His home seemed to them a grand place, but was little more than a long, low-roofed building. He protected them all from the occasional attack from strangers by having a fenced-in enclosure around the Manor House where livestock could be driven in for safety.

A larger hall had been built by 1377 on high ground affording even more protection from enemies and wild animals that still abounded in the area. Gradually tracks began to form ribbons of primitive roads on the landscape, connecting the outlying farms at the Dale, Summerhill and Sheepwash with the main village.

Each farm depended on the craftsmen who had begun to establish their trades locally. Roadside workshops appeared in the village with the craftsmen utilising those valuable minerals that were still being dug out of the ground around Whitehurst. Village life centred around the High Street, with an ale house at each end and farriers, ostlers and blacksmiths all working side-by-side.

Life in the 1400s was noisy and monotonous with the continuous ring of the hammer on the anvil penetrating even the thick walls of the ale house. The ale wife busily served tankards of rough ale to the blacksmiths customers as they rested against the upturned carts and waited for the horses to be shod.

In the late 1700s with the turnpiking of the major highways life became slightly easier for the farmers from the Bale Lane area, with roads kept in a reasonable state of repair. Toll houses began to appear with the Toll Keepers charging all that passed by. Cattle, sheep, horses and men, each had a different rate. His house, built at the corner of High Street in the late 1700s, was typical of Toll Gate houses, with a small window jutting to give the keeper a clear but dry place to collect his money and count the livestock as it passed by. The effect of a herd of beasts on their way to market must have made quite a sight as they passed the Malthouse Farm area, with villagers taking refuge in the ale house close by.

As the roads became better, so did the volume of traffic. This made the village blacksmith even busier, with ploughs and carts to repair and implements to make on the 'swage block', a rectangular block of cast iron with several holes for forming nails of different shapes. Among the most important tools made were the "Lazy Blacksmith" – a three-legged stand used to place the foreleg of the horse on while the ostler trimmed the animal's feet – and the branding irons, each with a distinctive mark to distinguish the livestock that roamed free in the fields around Godley Brook.

Although most farmers worked hard, some like Farmer Cartwright will be forever remembered for his sluggish and bad tempered attitude in ways and speech, which was said to have as much depth as the drone of the bees that swarmed around Stansmore Hall. The Drumble is said to have gained its name from the Anglo-Saxon word *Dran* meaning 'drone' and Cartwright's Drumble will always stay as a friendly reminder of days gone by.

World events had little effect on people who drank ale and lived in Dilhorne at the end of the 1700s. News took many months to reach the village by word of mouth as most people could neither read nor write, although they had a tiny school founded by the Earl of Huntingdon. There was little time for the ordinary child to have a formal education, with the need to know the weather by looking at the sky and knowing the best time to sow and gather being much more important.

The beginning of the 1800s brought many changes to the village. The All Saints Church, with its peel of six bells and rare octagonal tower had its nave and aisle rebuilt in 1819. A fine new stone-built hall was designed by Trubshaw of Great Haywood for the Buller family, who were Lords of the Manor and their memorials can still be seen inside the Church. A new school was built by the Marquis of Hastings in 1837.

The Old Parsonage still stands at the corner of Dilhorne Road and perhaps typifies a community where ale and religion have always gone together. The Colliers Arms where, according to Kelly's Directory, Mary Rigby was the licensee in 1840, stands opposite; though the name was changed in the 1980s to the very splendid Charlie Bassetts, in honour of one of the most popular inhabitants, it remains a landmark of the village. In the same directory, Daniel Inskip was a much-respected wheelwright, Joseph Salt was licensee of the Royal Oak as well as a coal master on Dilhorne Common, and Edward Jervis was Lord of the Manor.

The Gate House seems to be all that is left of the great hall whose fortunes failed when the last of the Buller family moved out in 1927. But, with careful investigation it is still possible to find some of the original stones that were used for building work around the village.

The sights around the Royal Oak have perhaps changed the most, with the blacksmith gone forever. The Toll House first changed to the Police House, then into a private house. The post office, where members of the Dale family attended to the telegraph messages for over 80 years, now provides tax forms for the motor car.

Perhaps one day, young people eager to get away from the hustle and bustle of the city life will find peace and quiet in this small out of the way village – and the young people of Dilhorne will no longer move to the cities. Next time you have an hour to spare, why not pause and while enjoying the most traditional of English pastimes – partaking of a refreshing pint. Try to discover some of the history that is all around you in the Royal Oak, Dilhorne.

DRAYCOTT

THE NEW PLOUGH

Although the 20th century is slowly eating away at the edges of the rural landscape of North Staffordshire, a few communities have managed to retain the heritage that was bestowed on them long ago. Draycott's history goes back to a time when farming was the most important industry, and a welcoming place to rest and take refreshment was a necessity after a hard day's toil.

The land where The New Plough stands fitted the bill then as now – with good food, fine ale and a reputation that has spread far beyond those ancient boundaries.

Over the years, the New Plough has seen many changes

The Roman Road from Newcastle to Rocester had finally fallen into disuse after the Legionnaires had moved on to colonise other parts of Britain. Anglo-Saxon settlements had begun to grow with possessions giving the ordinary people power. Owners of carts or drays were considered quite important, and they survived in small Cotes, grouped together to shelter them from the cold winds that blew across the open fields of Forsbrook.

Gradually the small group of dwellings began to form into hamlets and *Draege-Cote* began to grow. A simple Church was built and consecrated in 1268 and the tomb of Sir Richard Hugo De Dracot still remains inside. When these horses were released from their shafts they were hitched on the driving force of the instrument that all civilised life depends on, The Plough.

The monotonous country life was punctuated with simple events to celebrate the wonders of nature. One such was Plough Monday, which took place on the first Monday after January 6 and marked the beginning of the agricultural year. Bedecked with ribbons, the new plough was dragged along the lanes leading from Cheadle. It would have passed Rookery Farm, so jealously guarded from the Cromwellian soldiers, and across the track that went to Cresswell, with the plough boy always keeping St Margarets Church in view. The bell tower would have been ringing out in jubilation, as the plough passed the Ostlers house and came to rest at a farm and ale house before heading towards Blythe Bridge. Everyone the plough boy met was expected to contribute donations or largesse as well as rejoicing and singing.

As the years passed, the Harvest Supper became more important at the farms and ale houses, with the farmer's wife serving plates of sumptuous food and home-brewed beer in large quantities. In Kelly's Directory of 1840, listing the people who lived in the area, George Perry is named 'Licensee of the Draycott Arms and Farmer'.

Many old traditions have died out or changed beyond recognition, but the practice that began long ago with the purchase of a simple farm implement and the drinking of home-brewed beer has been passed down from generation to generation to become a tradition itself. Gradually, home brewing was replaced with mass-produced beer delivered in strong drays. But like this public house which over the years has seen many changes in both its name and appearance, the hospitality so evident in those far off days is still there in the shape of one of the most popular public houses in the area.

EAST VALE

THE SEA LION

Looking at most maps, it is hard to find East Vale. But, as soon as a visitor walks through the door of the Sea Lion Public House in Anchor Terrace, it is easy to see that the public spirit of the area is still very much alive.

Unlike many communities, East Vale's heritage does not go back to Roman times. The area came to life along with many other communities along with the soldiers who had returned from the Battle of Waterloo in 1840. The small groups of dwellings at Meir and Normacot were unable to cope with the young families that the pottery industry was calling out for. In the rural villages, there were only small cottages, most of which consisted of just one small room with an earth floor and open fire for cooking.

Many pottery manufacturers of the time began to have rows of houses built, first on the main road, then they began to fill the open ground towards Adderley Green with terraced houses, shops and drinking places. Some, by today's standards, were grim with names such as Hackett Place and Upper, Lower and Middle John Street all having the reputation of being the worst housing in the city. They were solidly built and most had a cooking range and a brown stone sink, but even the slightly better houses in Goddard Street and Anchor Terrace only had four rooms and an outside privy.

At the turn of the century, the pottery worker's life was hard dusty and long, with drinking one of the only social events enjoyed by most men.

The tower of the great St James Church, built in 1839 by Trubshaw and Johnson, could be seen by many inhabitants of East Vale. And the beautiful peel of bells could be heard, calling people to listen to sermons still echoing with the words spoken by the first Rector, The Reverend Benjamin Vale. But, many of the 600 seats would be empty as the lure of the public houses called out a stronger welcome to most people of East Vale.

The manufacture of cups and saucers, at factories such as Paragon, was hot and dusty and although the air in most public houses was thick with smoke from cigarettes and pipes, the words for friendly greetings would make the choking atmosphere bearable.

Perhaps it was partly due to the cigarettes that the mortality rate in East Vale was so high, with most men never reaching retirement age. But the peace gained from ten Woodbines was felt preferable to the risk that until recently was not made public.

The small shops that stood on most street corners greeted customers not only when they came in for 20 Capstan on pay day, but would willingly sell two Senior Service when money was scarce – which was particularly true after the Great War.

Cigarette butts were often picked up on a round trip to the herbalist at the top of Engine Bank (Bridgewood Street) to buy a small bottle of Syrup of Figs and then down the twisted lane about 200 yards along King Street, known by everyone as Hand Cuff Alley. These 'dog-ends' would sometimes be smoked straight from the ground with a match stick pushed in to help hold them. Most were carefully saved until a quiet moment at the bar of their favourite local, when the remains of the paper were removed and the unburnt tobacco was added to a tin of Old Holborn. This was then made into extremely thin "fags" as local people still call them (from the Anglo Saxon word Fag or Fagg – the end of something no one wants). Cigarettes were recycled with cigarette papers, a simple rolling machine, and an endless supply of Captain Webb matches because again and again these "Fags" would have to be relit due to their slender shape.

Only gradually did poverty and squalor disappear from the area between Meir Hay and Anchor Road. The pre-war building boom of the 1930s created modern housing, first in Leason Road then Sandon Road, Meir, with whole streets cleared in East Vale. Handcarts and barrows were used to transport what possessions each family had along unmade pavements. They would reluctantly pass the few public houses that were still open, and head towards the main road, trying hard to keep away from the tram tracks that ran along High Street to the brow of Meir Bank in Meir Lane. Although families settled well in their new surroundings and integrated well with other families that had been given the opportunity to live in the Meir, most never forgot their original neighbours and families from East Vale and often returned just to see how the area had first been cleared and then new houses built but just occasionally they found that the planners had saved little pieces like Goddard Street and the Sea lion although much altered nothing can destroy the friendly atmosphere that can only be found in the Sea Lion public house, East Vale.

Only a small area of East Vale remains

ETRURIA

THE CHINA GARDEN

The best way to describe the China Garden is a modern drinking place in a modern setting. The pub is as elegant as the area with discreet lighting, pleasant music and a patio that overlooks the marina. The noise from the busy road that runs alongside seems to melt away once inside the pub. Perhaps the vision that Josiah Wedgwood had in the 1700s to create a pleasant environment for his labourers which was home, workplace and somewhere to relax has nearly come true with the Festival Site: shops, offices and leisure facilities all accommodated on an area where once Shelton Bar belched smoke, noise and flames. When Shelton emptied the slag from its furnaces, the night sky would change to a brilliant red and the old folk would say: "The devil's in the clouds."

The rural landscape of North Staffordshire has undergone many changes over the years, with the old road from Leek to Sheffield once an ideal packhorse track, although the traders rarely paused to give the area between Wolstanton and Sneyd Green a second glance.

But families did choose to live along the main tracks, and Rushton Grange was one of the finest houses locally, with a history that dated from the time of the Domesday Survey. The Grange, a thatch-roofed building, stood facing Etruria Valley looking towards Wolstanton.

When the plague of the 1600s took its toll on the towns in Staffordshire, the occupants of the Grange had little defence; the whole family succumbed to that dreadful pestilence and without the workforce needed to give them proper burial in the churchyard, they were interned in one of the many pits that had been dug nearby. The plague was attributed to the Italian Governess Kate because of rat fleas found in her clothes; she was buried with her charges and it is said that even now her beautiful voice can be heard on a warm summer's night by visitors as they sit outside the China Garden.

The pure air of North Staffordshire breathed life into some great men in the 1700s, and none more so than those who were beginning to discover the potential of the clay so readily available in the ground.

As the industrial towns grew, so did the need for somewhere to escape to and so get away from the smoke and grime: the woods and small pools between the townships of Shelton and Basford were ideal. They chose the rural outskirts to build grand homes.

By the mid-1700s, Josiah Wedgwood had the great foresight to realise that the purchase of Ridgehouse Estate at Shelton would prove profitable. At the same time that he was creating pottery, James Brindley was making the transportation of goods easier with the use of canals. Great plans were set in motion to join the rivers Mersey and Trent.

The Hall and Park created by Josiah Wedgwood were grand places, with lakes for fishing in the summer and skating in the snow-covered winters. Villagers on the 350 acre estate that Wedgwood built lived quite well and worked hard to produce ware which Josiah called Etruscan. He thought this was an ideal name for the community and Etruria was born. This village was probably one of the first purpose-built estates in England, Port Sunlight is one of the few others.

Shelton even had its own racecourse, boasting a grandstand. It was visited by thousands during Wakes Week and the last meeting there was on 5th August 1840. Then, Earl Granville sank shafts on the site and the resultant colliery was known as The Racecourse. The pit closed in 1941 because of severe flooding.

Very little remains of those days. The Roundhouse, the canal, tow paths, bridges and Etruria Hall, though extensively changed, still have some of the original feel about them. As with most communities, many tales and stories have been passed down from previous generations, keeping some of the history intact for generations to come, with tales of ancestral homes in Stoke travelling the Atlantic to Wisconsin.

Desperate families from the area emigrated to America in the 1840s, due to the unemployment caused by the increased use of machinery in the factories. Descendants of those families, who began that perilous journey by catching a final glimpse of Josiah's home and the newly-built steel works by the canal side, still live in the lovely town of Pottersville today.

Although much of the language of the early Etrurians has been absorbed into modern speech, just occasionally a word or phrase crops up that brings back memories of a time long gone. "Bogies Dean" is a phrase that once breathed fear into the hearts of everyone who worked at Shelton Bar in the 1800s. This demigod claimed human sacrifices at a disturbing rate and poor families were often robbed of their fathers when the Bogie Truck proved difficult to move. A simple memorial service held where the worker was last seen was the only comfort the family had.

Another word that has caused great controversy over the years is 'Macalonies', an area somewhere in the locality of the China Garden. The origin of its name has over the years led to much speculation. Was the

Festival Park marina. A modern pub in a modern setting.

word a tongue-in-cheek corruption of Macaroni, from the groups of Italian immigrants who would gather by the bridge over the canal to talk of their homeland? Was it perhaps just how local children would talk of their favourite place, a marshy canal, where wild life abounded and children could learn to swim in the warm holes where industrial water entered the canal? Was the answer as simple as the name printed on the bridge, McElhone of Glasgow? Each person has their own answer to what the Macca was.

Other local areas included Timikees, Vee Banks, Shord-ruck and Jelly land; these are just a few of the places that remain only as a fond memory, along with Shelton Bar which breathed its last fiery breath in 1971 and the Wedgwood factory which moved to Barlaston in the 1930s, with the final link severed in 1950.

The transformation of the Festival Site has given new life to an area which was beginning to succumb to centralisation of factories, and the canal is an added bonus for the boats that call into the marina. With the foundation laid down so many years ago by Josiah Wedgwood it would be impossible to do anything else but share in the magic he found at Etruria.

FEGG HAYES

THE JESTER

The sign outside the Jester Public House mirrors the image that people have of the small area between Great Chell and Oxford (a Council estate almost enclosed by the once-huge spoil heaps from Chatterley Whitfield colliery), known by locals and visitors alike as Fegg Hayes. This area is often the butt of many people's jokes. The name itself sets it apart from its neighbours, outsiders often think someone long ago played a cruel trick on the first residents. Why call areas Whitfield and Westcliffe by easily understandable names and then call the shaded ground between them "Fegg Hayes"? However, if the words are taken back to their original Anglo-Saxon beginnings a different light can be put on the area.

The old Anglo-Saxon word 'Hayes' describes the small woods that once covered the area, while that wonderfully descriptive word 'Fegg' simply means rough end. If the area had been called Woodend would people remember it as well? Maybe not. Perhaps this is one of the

Fegg Hayes: industrial skyline

reasons that many residents have a rich sense of humour that is known throughout the city.

Quite a cross section of people frequent the Jester, from those who use its well-lit bar to meet old friends and to share conversation, to others who use the quiet corners to look at the job prospects in the early edition of the Evening Sentinel picked up from the nearby newsagent. Before long, the pages are turned over to the sports reports.

One eagerly-scanned report that is not often in the paper, but enjoyed in many of the older parts of Fegg Hayes, is what the Homing Pigeons are doing this season. Pigeons have long been kept in lofts and sheds in the back yards of the terraced houses. Over many years the sight of a flight of pigeons has made quite a spectacle as they swoop and swirl over the Bowling Green.

Not everyone has the same affection for these birds. Wash-day in Fegg Hayes before the invention of the tumble dryer was often punctuated by exclamations of dismay as the clean washing blowing in the spring air had to be re-washed, after it had unfortunately become the target of the pigeons on their way home. And the Primary School roof was turned a speckled white, standing as it does on the flight path between the open ground towards Turnhurst and the birds' home-base. Not only were these birds kept for sport, but many people depended on them as a supplement to their wages. Perhaps some of the tales that for many years went round the Jester best describe the affinity that man has with pigeons.

One tale was of Old Nobby, whose small wage was unfortunately consumed in best draught Guinness on a Friday night. Unable to face the prospect of no Sunday dinner, he sold two of his best homing birds to a visitor from Tunstall on Saturday lunchtime. Sad to see them go, but with a sly smile, Nobby set off to purchase a small piece of mutton from the Co-op, then on to his home in the Withington Road area. By Sunday evening he had a good meal inside him and welcomed the birds back to their loft.

Other tales include the ingenious wife of Bazzer who managed to prepare a delicious, if not slightly strange "chicken" pie when money was scarce to feed her hungry family. After spending an hour consoling the head of the house on the loss of two of his best pigeons, she assured him that she would keep a closer eye on them in future.

Another tale that is saved for special occasions at the Jester is that of Mick, a former sailor from Ireland. Because of his failing eyesight, he went around the area where the clinic now stands with a silver blue pigeon on his shoulder; the locals were too amused to tell him that his beloved parrot had succumbed to the fish shop cat.

Although there is much humour in Fegg Hayes there is a serious side to the area. This was once a mining village amid several collieries, but many young people now go to the large towns for a night out or to find work, which in turn gives them the opportunity to live away from the streets and roads that all lead to the Biddulph Road. Perhaps one day Fegg Hayes, like many other small communities, will disappear; but hopefully what will not disappear are the memories and, like Nobby's pigeons, no matter where they go when home calls they have to return.

FENTON

THE DUKE OF WELLINGTON

Arnold Bennett might have forgotten the town and most commuters hardly give it a second glance as they speed along the busy A50 towards Stoke. The families that have lived in the area around the Duke of Wellington public house have always loved 'Fen-Town' – possibly called because the early settlement was close to the muddy area by the river Trent; *Fenny* is the old word for 'muddy surface'. However, *Feun-tun* can also mean 'enemy town'.

When the Domesday survey was undertaken, Alward owned all the land on the outskirts of Heron Cross and gradually, through marriages, the land was passed down from the daughter of Vivian the Rector of Stoke in the 1100s to the Biddulphs. In 1564 it was sold again to John Brode. Most of these family names have long been forgotten as the tidal wave of houses engulfed the small townships. Others remain as a memorial to the past.

Fenton Vivian: all that's left of Fenton Low

'Lane Delph' or Middle Fenton probably gained its name from the Ironstone china patented by Charles James Mason in 1873, so reminiscent of the china made in the Delph area of Holland. While the tranquil area by the river known as Mount Pleasant was famous for its rural feel right up to the mid-1800s, with Fenton Hall standing opposite the Great Mansion built for Thomas Whieldon. All that is left of Fenton Vivian is a street name, and Fenton Low is only a friendly way of referring to the Fenton Park area; but, with careful investigation, traces of the former moated farm houses can be found.

One of the inhabitants of the area in the 1800s was a Henry Warrington who owned Berry Hill works as well as farming 400 acres. Another was Joseph Myatt, whose factory was where, in the late 1800s, John Wesley, on his last journey to preach gave a rousing talk to the miners and potters.

One of the many inhabitants of Great Fenton Hall in the 1800s was a William Hancock who lived with his brother-in-law, potter John Locket, for some time. William, both a hot water engineer and iron-founder, supplied, in 1851, cast-iron lamp posts in the area. One of his sons, John, was secretary of the Fenton Athenaeum, a society set up as part of the new urban culture of the Victorian middle classes.

By the end of the 1800s, Fenton was changing fast, with the many public houses all busy with an ever increasing number of workers. One of the most popular public houses in Fenton was on the site now occupied by the Duke of Wellington. Although this modern pub has, in recent years, undergone major refurbishing, the tradition built up by licensees such as the one noted in Kelly's directory of 1840 as J. Johnson is still evident. The men who were employed in the factories that had begun to spring up along Victoria Road and City Road enjoyed nothing better after a hard day's work than to stand on sawdust-covered floors, with spittoons on hand to get rid of some of the factory dust, left elbow on the bar and right arm supporting a pint of best mild. Gradually, ladies were allowed into this once male-dominated domain though not in the public bar; more usually, they sat in the snug with a port and lemon. With no bar meals, it was a few cold lamb sandwiches brought from home, to be shared with the neighbours, while sitting in their "own" seats in the crowded room.

Even this changed, as people began to seek better drinking places, with pubs becoming ultra modern, snacks supplied in as many forms as there once were people. Even the terraced houses, out-buildings and coal sheds, where many a drinking session ended, have disappeared.

The name of Foley, once a completely separate township, derives from the low lying ground and the tendency the area had of holding the smells associated with the countryside. It has now undergone a complete transformation, with Foley Place perhaps one of the best examples of the work done by modern architects who have tried to maintain the feel of the mid-1800s. But the station has gone, and all that remains of the once grand Manor house is a gate post and the name given to the swimming pool.

Foley Place

One of the many inhabitants of this new Fenton was the young Michael John Bettaney. He grew up in the William Street area in the mid-1950s and, after attending various schools throughout the city, he went on to gain a second class honours degree in English in 1972, at Pembroke College. Many conversations went on long into the night at the Duke of Wellington public house about the charge of spying, for which he was convicted in the mid-1980s.

New Fenton has spread out far beyond the old boundaries to include all the separate townships, with the fine Albert Square and war memorial shining like a beacon to all who pass. A Sixth Form College has risen from the foundations laid down by the Victorian builders of Fenton Manor.

All this has brought changes to the lives of the people who use the Duke of Wellington, but those born within the sights and sounds of this pub still have a soft spot for Fenton.

FORD GREEN

THE FORD INN

'The Ford' is a comparatively new name; previously, it was 'The Railway Hotel' because of the small station near to it. The railway itself was a mineral line serving the Norton Colliery, Robert Heath's iron works both there and in Biddulph, and the Chatterley Whitfield Colliery; it also carried a few commuters.

Did the yeomen farmers who first worked the ground between Norton and Smallthorne have any idea that, in over 700 years, people would still be fascinated by their lives?

The first reference to the actual land is a family deed of 1412 which contains the following lines: "Thomas De Thursfiede of Whitfielde gives and confirms to Richard Heir of Sibbille Del Forde a parcel of land including a green at Smallthorne adjacent to the Trent." From then on, the Ford family owned the land, including where the present Hall is now situated, although the building that is standing today was probably built on the ground where the first wooden one stood.

At this point the question arises: is it coincidental that an ordinary family called Ford chose to live by the place where the Bank Hay Brook was narrow enough to be forded, or did the family give the area its name? No one can be certain. Either way, a small family community had begun to grow by the 1500s, with a few shelters for the serfs and borders, while the new landowners were beginning to grow affluent enough to build fairly grand homes. The house between the main track that led from the villages towards Endon and the trading towns that were beginning to grow, was typical of the buildings that appeared throughout the country in the mid-1500s. These were mainly wooden, with local materials being used where possible. Although it had to undergo the degradation of becoming practically derelict before someone saw it for what it was, it has managed to retain many of its original features.

With a little time and some careful examination, evidence can be uncovered about some of the ordinary people who worked in the area around the Ford Inn and its famous neighbouring Hall. Although the area had what we now call a hall, it was little more than a simple two-storied building, and there was little else. Many acres of land were still uncultivated with animals allowed to roam free. The people who lived in the hall were farmers who, through marriage and good business deals, were slowly gaining property and wealth.

These newly-rich gentry were able to employ skilled workers from outside the area to make their living accommodation as fine as the building techniques of the time would allow. These workmen, like those of today, would often leave mementoes of their presence as if to mark the work they were so proud of, stating that they were not just ordinary people. The inscription over the entrance to the hall gives Raphe Sutton Carpenter the immortality that even the owners of the great pyramids would have liked; and the names of James Oaks and Hezehiah Harrison from Steandey can still be read, inscribed on the windows of the parlour chamber, along with the date, July 1790, as if to remind people that although the centuries have passed their workmanship will remain.

These men and many others would have enjoyed the hospitality of the people who lived in the area, probably lodging at one of the smaller farms along the track that is now known as Ford Green Road. Doubtless they drank home-brewed ale and mead made with honey from the bees that were kept by many people.

By the mid-1700s, work had already been undertaken to renovate the hall, with the family probably moving out for a short time. This gave the alehouses and farms a greater opportunity to grow rich, with tradesmen pausing just long enough to spend their money and perhaps barter some of their wares in exchange for good home-cooked food.

Although the interior of Ford Green Hall that the visitor sees today seems to the untrained eye typical of a house of the 1500s, it contains no original furniture, which is quite logical, as furniture was replaced as and when it was worn out or outdated. Some furniture was passed down from father to son and often some of the larger pieces were mentioned in wills and legacies. This gives historians a clearer picture of what our forebears considered important. One of the main items of value in wills seemed to be beds and bedsteads. The bed in the Parlour Chamber once belonged to the Deane family of Norton Hall and was made in the 1600s. The one that the Ford family owned was less grand and had a feather mattress.

Ford Green Hall is steeped in history; as the oldest house in Stoke-on-Trent, there are stories to tell if intrigue, death and valour. One other claim to fame was the Iron Works that once stood opposite to the Hall. It became world famous for the chains it forged – the row of houses opposite the hall was known as Chain Row. Also, the ironwork that supports the mighty bridge across the Menai Straits came from here. Many experienced workers came to Ford Green from South Staffordshire and local lads earned their pocket money by fetching buckets of ale for the perspiring forge men from the Railway Hotel (now The Ford) and other nearby inns.

Ford Green Hall

The view of the Hall that people who use the Ford Inn see nowadays is of a gable-ended building, with outbuildings including a fine example of a brick dove-cote built about the middle of the 1700s. The renovation of the hall has taken many years of hard work by the National Trust who purchased the house in 1948. Although hampered by the never ending threat of the nearby brook flooding and ever-increasing costs, they have managed to give the visitor a clear indication of a time long gone.

Most people who walk along the road do so for two reasons: some simply call at the pub, but then visit the hall; and visitors to the hall more often than not call into the Ford Inn for a drink. Hopefully, those who use the Ford Inn will continue to be ordinary folk, going about their lives making history every day.

FORSBROOK

THE BUTCHERS ARMS

With a delightful outdoor relaxation area and a friendly atmosphere, the Butchers Arms has all that is required of a modern public house. But the Blythe Brook, running beside the large car park, has long been used by both people and animals who have paused to take refreshment from its cool clear water as it gently meanders on its never ending trek to the sea.

Bears and wild cats were among the first visitors to the brook, even before man discovered its beneficial qualities, taking refuge in the comparative safety of the area around Callowhill Wood. These and many other creatures drank and fought for survival on the ground where the Butchers Arms now stands.

The Roman legionnaires arrived in approximately 200 AD; they always kept away from marshy land, preferring if possible the high ridges, also making a straight road from their fort at Newcastle. They also carved a salt road from the Cheshire Plains through Werrington and Caverswall. Soldiers with salt filled panniers rested just long enough to take a cooling drink at the brook before heading to Draycott, then on to Tean arriving at the fort at Rocester.

By 400 AD, main settlements were beginning to flourish. Slowly, as the families grew, small villages began to appear on the landscape around Caverswall.

The clear waters of the Blythe

One chief, by the name of Fotes, made his small settlement beyond Dilhorne, where the fresh water brook crossed the road, fish and animals could be caught and trapped to supplement their meagre diet.

Because of territorial fights, Swain had become the leader of the scattered groups by 900 and although fierce and warlike, his lazy attitude held Fotes settlement by the Broc (brook) behind the growing settlement of Caverswall and Cheadle.

The Domesday Book does not mention the settlement beside the brook. The village people had little to call their own. The only possession that most of them had was probably a wooden or horn cup which they used for both eating and drinking. But they fared better than those who lived towards the boundary – at least they had fresh water to drink.

Gradually time passed and village life became better. With fertile land around Mount Pleasant the farm labourers in 1400 enjoyed nothing better than to share bread, cheese and a little home brewed beer with the farm labourers from Caverswall in the area where Eastbank Ride now stands.

As the feud between the King and Parliament grew in the 1600s it was ordered that the Totmonslow Hundred, of which one of the settlements was *Fox-brok*, had to train and exercise 135 foot soldiers and 35 carbines. All this had quite an effect on such a small community; the few who were left to tend the fields looked on in dismay as the Puritan soldiers broke down crops, smashed wooden fences and polluted the clear brook with filth-covered horses as they galloped to their garrison at Caverswall.

Joviality and idleness were forbidden in Puritan England, with ale houses forced to close. The villagers of Forfboc (Forsbrook) found little to smile about, even the brook was covered with snow that winter, which made life practically impossible. Only the glow from the smoking fires in the shelters gave any comfort to them, but even collecting fuel was made difficult around Dilhorne Road for those who had failed to have a fuel store. Sticks were frozen and the peat was undiggable.

Spring came eventually and the ford that straggled the road bubbled with life. New settlers came and landowners were only too eager to take advantage of the arable land. New farms began to shape the village and, although most of the villagers still lived in thatched huts near the brook, the landowners had grand block-built buildings. Forsbrook Hall still stands as it did in the time of Charles II.

When the main trading roads were turnpiked, travelling to the markets became easier. Forsbrook Tollgate House stood at the corner of Dilhorne Road and Cheadle Road in 1838, and the area became a good place to rest and take advantage of the fresh water for the livestock and ale and food to feed the people. So fast was the evolution of this tiny village however that the Toll House closed only 40 years later.

The beautiful St Peters Church, built by Mr Goldstraw of Wetley Rocks, took approximately two years to complete and was consecrated in 1849 leading the way to a better Forsbrook.

The Square, which in the late 1800s was little more than two dirt tracks, contained a small cottage in the middle. And the Grand Temperance Hall urged people from the evils of strong drink, which was quite difficult with the four pubs that the village boasted at the turn of 1900. The Bulls Head and Miners Arms have disappeared, with the Roebuck now standing by a fine road bridge instead of the ford. The Butchers Arms has altered slightly but remains as solid as ever.

Over the years many once-familiar landmarks have gone. The cottage in the Square was demolished in 1905, the Temperance Hall, built in memory of Minnie Eileen Grimwade, was demolished in 1927. Even the Toll House, once so important to the village, made way in 1960 for the modern houses of York Close and Portland Drive.

Of the many people who have visited Forsbrook some have rested on their journeys, while others have made Forsbrook their home, bringing with them new ideas and changes to the village.

Only the brook has remained unchanged and, if people who cross over the bridge on their way to visit the Butchers Arms take a few minutes to look into the clear water, just maybe they might see a reflection of the past.

HALMEREND

THE RAILWAY INN

Travelling as most people do, noting little of the small sign post, it is quite easy to miss the Railway Inn, Halmerend, signalling people to slow down and stoke up their fuel tanks before carrying on to Audley. The trains that once steamed customers into the Railway Inn are now no more than just a distant memory, but with a little help Halmerend may become more than just one insignificant spot on a map.

A slight indication of who the first residents were is obvious from the dialect spoken and the naming of the settlement. The fertile ground, the projecting piece of land the shelters stood on, and the fact that it was at the end of the other group of dwellings caused the Norse people cause to call it Hals-Ende.

Some people will say the reason the older residents of the area still speak with a slightly different dialect is that there are still traces of the Old English people in them. Some phrases may seem strange to those who live beyond the ancient boundaries of Stoke-on-Trent, but translation can be asked for at the Railway Inn

There is little mention of the immediate area in the Domesday Book, but as with most Saxon villages, Halmende (Halmerend) people were busy eking out a living on the land with the serfs never venturing further than Alsagers Bank and Hayes Wood.

The Hearth Tax Returns of 1666 suggest the number of people in the village. There were 30 households recorded; Mrs Norton, Messrs Boulton, Catherake, Sillitoe and Whitehall were some notable residents who would be quite 'sneeped' if they were ignored as they walked along the lanes towards Miles Green.

By 1700, land owning was an important part of the economy, with the villagers doffing their caps as Master Tollet passed by on his way to the Red House that he had purchased in 1751.

When Richard Parrot spoke in the 1700s of Halmerend he noted the homes had no land of their own only gardens where 'taters' and 'choniks' could be grown to help fill the saucepan which hung over the fire. A warming pan of Lobby was the staple diet of the tanners, thatchers, websters and ground colliers who made up the trades of the men of the village.

Domestic industry was beginning to flourish and gradually nail making provided employment for many families. The availability of iron made Staffordshire the centre of the industry. The process was very hot, smoky and dirty, and a sup of ale at the end of the day was the best way to clear the dust off the chest of the workers. The nails would be taken to Hanley Market in sturdy carts to be sold for the industries that were being set up in Cheshire and Lancaster. This gave the people of Halmerend a good living and money to spend.

Halmerend entered the steam age with style in the late 1800s. The clatter of wheels and sharp screech of the whistle pierced the early morning air. Those workers who were 'franked' would be seen scurrying along the High Street with their 'snapping' tucked under their arms as the steam train crossed over the road to enter Halmerend Station.

Official census forms from 1801 onwards give a clear indication of the population of the village. The general increase coincided with the growth of coal production. Colliers were some of the best customers of the beer houses in the area, being able to distinguish the quantity of the brew by the 'yed' (head) on it. Although coal-mining has always been one of the most important trades, it is also one of the most dangerous, with the customers of the beer houses in the area sharing in the sorrows of the many disasters that occurred.

When Halmerend National School was opened in 1849, many of the pinafored schoolgirls could be seen skipping along the tracks from the Hollins Farm area. Many had large white ribbons to hold their hair up to stop them, as their Mams would say, from going 'Sken-eyed'. While cloth capped boys, with catapults at the ready to fire at any passing rabbits, could be seen jumping Dean Brook. A bigger school was soon needed and Halmerend Council School was built on the same site in 1913.

Many other buildings began to appear along the roads in the 1900s. The Congregation Chapel was used as a mortuary for the bodies of 155 men and boys who lost their lives in the dreadful disaster at the Minnie Pit in 1918; there is a memorial opposite the Chapel, but it has been vandalised in recent years. The Chapel became one of the most popular places for social events: potted beef sandwiches on best china muffins were served with hot tea from a big Brown Betty tea pot supplied by the Chapel Ladies.

By 1939 the need for a better education for the older children was called for. The children from Alsager Bank School and those from the outlying areas near Quarry Farm joined the children from Halmerend School, bringing a few pieces for their dinner. Their new school became Halmerend Senior Mixed with Mr W. Bower the head teacher. Any of the girls he caught being 'peevish' to the younger ones in the playground would get told-off and any boy who called out "ow-at" instead of "Good-morning Sir" would get the cane.

The 1900s brought many changes to Halmerend, with the motor car becoming more common and road travel easier. Many people tended to avoid the twisting B5367 road and thereby missed Halmerend altogether, but the village remained quite industrious with its own shops. W. M. Riley's ironmonger, seedsman and furniture dealer looked after some of the larger requirements, as well as making sure the post was on time.

The Co-op attended to the everyday needs. The errand boy arriving early to 'tickle' the fire and make sure the 'ess-hole' was clear before the white coated, bow-tied manager gave him his daily tasks. Stacking tins of Spam, spreading sawdust on the shop floor and making sure that

Halmerend

there was a dark wood, straight-backed chair available for the lady customers while they deliberated on how much loose tea and tub butter was needed. Only after this would the lad make his daily deliveries on his bicycle along Station Road, past the Railway Inn, towards the farms. His straw basket piled high with orders.

Even this has changed now, with most people choosing to do their shopping at Silverdale and beyond. Hopefully, Halmerend will never lose the individuality that sets it apart and visitors to the Railway Inn will take time to listen to the locals as they call a friendly "ay-up duck, ast avin a drink".

HANFORD

THE BULL'S HEAD

Standing on the corner of Bankhouse Road and New Inn Lane, the Bull's Head Hotel calls people to its pleasantly lit rooms and relaxed atmosphere. With a little encouragement and the offer of another glass of bitter, a talkative evening will often begin. The conversation always starts gently and builds up to exaggerated tales of bigger, better and more unusual examples of life. Many colloquialisms used today by regulars as they sit around the solid tables in the shining bar have, like the river that meanders its way through Hanford, filtered their way through the area's history and here perhaps is the origin of just one:

Like most communities the first settlers to the area built their shelters not far from the water's edge, probably near the land where Northwood farm stands. In the time of the Domesday Book the fast running Lyme Brook emptied itself into the yet-unpolluted Trent as it ran its course, in the area where Hanford Bridge crossed the rough track. This supplied the fresh food needed to supplement the meagre diet for the Hamlet by the Ford, gradually the village of *Ham-ford* grew.

Village life by the 1400s was mundane but orderly, with the inhabitants trying to grow enough food not just for themselves but some to take along Stone Road to the market at Newcastle. Slowly strange new foods were beginning to filter in from the New World. Potatoes became the staple part of Hanford's economy by the mid-1600s but, when the potato blight swept across the countryside, Hanford people began to realise that unless they diversified, their growing families would starve.

Barley grew in the open field of Whitmore and this, like the wheat grown around the Sideway area, was untouched by the blight. After these crops were harvested and thrashed at the primitive mill, they were mixed with spring water and allowed to ferment in the warm kitchen where bread was browning in the ovens.

The sweet smell of fermenting ale and fresh bread would encourage passers-by to pause to take refreshment to sustain them on their journey. Many of these simple people who frequented these first ale houses would be enthralled by tales from the owners, thereby encouraging them to call again.

One farmer who lived in the area told tales of his visit south, and of the fabulous animals he encountered in cages in the Parkland of London.

Just another far-fetched story?

Animals at least twice as large as the Bull that he was once so proud of. Some of those strange creatures he saw had short legs, tough skins and a giant horn in the centre of their heads. So immense were these creatures, that it was hard to describe or compare them to the head of his beloved bull which he displayed on the wall of his home.

Over the road, the farmer who kept the best fighting cocks in the area spoke of the things he encountered on his travels north. Great mountains where the snow never melted and strange mixture of food cooked in a sheep's stomach lining, of a musical instrument like a cloth bag with spikes and fierce men in strange skirts.

As with most men with a good tale to tell, these two farmers became well known for their extravagant tales, with local people egging them on by first going to the farm with the fighting cocks, then over the road to the Bulls Head Ale House to see if the second farmer could outdo the first tale. These two houses began to be known far and wide as the places where fanciful tales were told and a great rivalry built up between the men.

By the late 1700s, the mill at Hanford had changed from working the corn to grinding flint and gradually the simple farms disappeared to be replaced by modern houses and shops. In fact very little remains of those far-off days, and perhaps the Bulls Head Hotel gives a slight indication of where one of the farms might have stood. What has remained is the phrase to describe a story so far fetched that it is hard to believe; and perhaps like this tale, it is just a "Cock and Bull" story!

HANLEY

THE FRENCH HORN

In stark contrast to the busy shopping centre across the square, The French Horn evokes a genteel view of times past. How many visitors today pausing to admire a tiny piece of Hanley realize that the land around the French Horn was used long before Hanley became what it is today, a busy shopping complex. With a little imagination some of that long gone history can be unearthed, making your visit to The French Horn even more interesting.

The area still abounds with characters

Although primitive Stone Age Man had begun the long struggle to control his environment, it was not until the Roman invasion in approximately 200 AD that civilised people began to populate Britain.

The Legionnaires who marched across the country to their fort at Newcastle found the steep-sided valley between the River Trent and its tributary the Fowlea particularly inhospitable. They left the land alone, probably calling it *bassus* or "low area"; maybe Basford gained its name this way.

By 400 AD, waves of land-hungry warriors had begun to travel the coast line of England looking for inlets. When the River Trent became unnegotiable they abandoned their crafts and pushed inland until they found suitable settlement grounds. With little resistance, the Anglo Saxon invaders could choose the best land, leaving the other areas to the natives who had begun to make their primitive shelters in the clefts of the hills. Perhaps the Clough area was left as a reminder of those people.

The small groups of dwellings were beginning to spread out to form settlements by the year 900, but the land was hard to cultivate. With damp and boggy ground man and beast took great care where he rested, always trying to avoid the marshes.

Gradually these small groups of settlements or towns, from the Latin *tyran*, began to alter the view. Some encampments were built at the top of the hills, some by the villas, left deserted by the Roman occupation, some sheltered by the hills and some by the lee of the high ridges; Shelton, Trent Vale, Talke and Hanley had been born.

A grant was conferred by the crown to Richard, the son of Noel of Han-ley (later Hanley) in 1227. The enclosure of dwellings was beginning to grow at a steady rate. The township of Hanley was able to provide a foot-soldier to the Castle for 40 days in war time. This soldier's job was the envy of his kin-folk whom he met as he paused to repair his armour at the *fundo* area of Hanley. Out of this Latin word grew two words that are common place today, Foundry and Fountain, both mean the same – to pour out. This is probably when the area first became a primitive staging post, with refreshing horn cups of ale supplied to the King's men.

The great trading towns of the South began to grow by the 1600s. It took many weeks to make the long journey from the industrial north, and the people of Hanley provided the food and drink needed to refresh those weary travellers. But the area had no fresh water for the livestock, therefore it became an expensive commodity. By the mid-1600s the area had been cleared and wooden thatched buildings were being built. Hovels for men, shelters for beasts. Flagons of rough ale were served, brewed from barley grown on the fertile lands towards Endon and yeast, a by-product of the thriving bakery industry.

Much bartering went on, with goods exchanging hands and the country-dwellers becoming quite prosperous out of the traders. Ale, bread, animal fodder and fresh water were exchanged for cloth, nails fancy goods and even a little of the newly discovered tobacco. These in turn were sold to the inhabitants of Hanley, first from carts grouped together, then small shops began to appear, clustered around the ale houses. Traders began to come from the surrounding villages to take advantage of Hanley's great market days.

After the Battle of Waterloo many soldiers brought home mementoes of that great war in France to be displayed in the ale houses. Guns, swords, flags and even the battered French Horn all had their place as, long into the night, heroes sat around the tables drinking tankards of ale and telling tales.

The pottery industry was gradually changing, rural landscapes with primitive kilns appearing on every corner. John Mare's factory was built in the late 1700s, although in Miles Bank with few other buildings in the area, his kilns would have extended well over Fountain square. By the early 1800s, any trace of rural England had gone forever from the townships of Hanley. It was decided to remove the stagnant water at Had-ley Pond in front of the covered shed built as a market hall in 1819.

However, all this prosperity brought in a rougher element, with the area between the Swan Public House and the French Horn renowned as a place where bawdiness and drunkenness were common. Stern punishments were meted out and, although little written evidence remains, records still exist of the three men, who in 1820 were convicted of the assault of a young woman in the area around the square and hanged for their crime at Stafford Gaol. They were buried in Hanley churchyard – ironically, near to Swan Passage, as if to add to their punishment.

Lesser crimes were dealt with by the Reverend John Middleton who had two methods: women were placed in a chair over the pool and dunked, while the men were made to sit in front of the congregation on Sunday. Both these methods proved unsuccessful, whether because of the effects of the ale or the sermon is not recorded, but most slept through their punishments.

The area abounded with characters at this time. One well known within the vicinity of the French Horn was "Easy Bear" who appears to have spent some time stuck to a greased pole but he, along with the pole, has long gone.

In 1845 a new Town Hall was completed and the whole area was given a face lift. By 1840 a paved area was created around the French Horn and a fresh water fountain was erected. The Town Hall was replaced in the mid-1880s by the building that was known as the Queen's Hotel in Albion Square. The Victoria Hall was added to the rear in 1887-1889.

Most of the streets in Hanley housed at least one brewery and, in Wards History of 1840, it was said that there were 45 licensed inns, liquor shops or victualing houses and nearly 100 beer houses in the town. Some of the most well-known were in this area and, although The Golden Lion, The Angel, The Grapes, The Lamb and The Swan have all gone, their memories have been saved to pass on to the few drinking places that remain.

Of some of the other businesses that were thriving in Fountain Square in the late 1800s, one was Mrs Appleby's post office which occupied a small room in the square, with a Mr Timmis' business next door.

After Sebastopol had fallen and the hostilities in France had ended in 1855 Hanley joined in the peace celebrations. Mr Wm. Jones, the butcher, provided an ox for roasting in the square, and the market was overflowing with people from far and wide, joining in the jubilations.

By the late 1800s the staff at the Town Hall found it quite a difficult job to balance the books of such a prosperous township and it was up to the Borough Accountants of the time, Geo. Barlow, to make the final decision on how the money was best spent.

The end of the century was graced by a local lady whose voice could be heard in Music Halls all over the country – Gertie Gitana. Though she was born in Longport in 1888, her family moved to Hanley when she was 3. She retired from the stage in 1938 and died in London in 1957. Frederick Street was then renamed in her honour to Gitana Street.

As the new century dawned, so did great changes to Hanley, with pubs being demolished almost daily to make way for bigger and better shops. Gradually, the Hanley that our great-grandfathers knew was disappearing. Like poor Mr Holland who, in 1903 on his way home from a Band of Hope meeting singing "When the roll is called in Heaven, I'll be there" was summoned to his maker in John Street. The earth opened and he disappeared into one of the many disused pit shafts. After extensive investigations, no trace was found of him and a simple memorial service was given on the spot where he was last seen.

As another century draws near, the face of Hanley will probably change again, but hopefully the planners will keep this small corner of the past. Hanley once bustled with characters that have all but disappeared; only memories and tales remain, but with the help of the friendly people of Hanley, a welcome will be given to everyone at The French Horn.

HARTSHILL

THE NOAH'S ARK

The grand building standing at the top of Hartshill Bank has only slight similarities to its namesake, with the porch doors just wide enough to allow people to go in two by two. Although standing on high ground, it is not tossed about in a wilderness but firmly anchored on all sides by the trappings of the 20th century.

With houses behind, a bank and medical institute opposite, a post office and small shop on each side, it is easy to see why this Noah's Ark is one of the busiest drinking places around.

Whereas the original Ark went forward to create a new future, by going back in time, some of the reasons that people come from miles around to discover the hospitality of the Noahs Ark may be discovered.

The congestion of the roads today denies most people the enjoyment of that wonderful climb from Stoke – past the Convent and School of St Dominic's and the houses that seem to have grown from the hillside. When the summit is reached there is that wondrous view of the industrial parts of Etruria to be marvelled at, a view that can only be bettered by a clear night and the lights of Cliff Vale.

In 1866 the then Prince of Wales laid the foundation stone of what was to become the hospital complex; this brought work to the fading area around the Noah's Ark. Under advice from Florence Nightingale, a revolutionary pavilion system was built at the hospital on the Mount Estate – perhaps by today's standards antiquated, but this was to mark a new start in medicine.

Fire was a frequent occurrence in the mid-1800s with both the Noahs Ark and the Holy Trinity Church suffering greatly, not only from the fires but also lack of an efficient water supply. George Gilbert designed the beautiful Holy Trinity Church under the direction of Herbert Minton, with Minton's home in 1842 being a Longfield cottage. The great church building and grounds were to become the centre of a new community, with a beautiful dado in the nave commemorating in memorial tiles the lives of some of the great people of Hartshill.

This was a busy time for builders in the area with the Mount being important enough to be mentioned in Wards Directory of the time. Lower down the road, the house built by John Tomlinson was typical of the two-storey buildings of the time. Cliff Vale later became known throughout the city as St Dominic's School. At the same time, Herbert Minton was building cottages for his workers on both sides of the main road, with remnants of some of these still to be seen today.

The Orthopaedic Hospital, with its modern facilities, still has a few remnants of its former life as Longfield cottage where, in 1826, Dinah Maria Mullock was born. She became better known, after her marriage, as Mrs Craik, author of 'John Halifax, Gentleman'.

Stoke registers of 1738 mentions Hartshill as a group of dwellings although many of these were at the lower end of Hartshill Road. With the high fields of Hartshill open for animals both wild and domestic to roam free, the area around the Noah's Ark was noted for red squirrels. Few of these are left, as the grey ones that were brought in are far more aggressive.

In those far-off days, the drinking habits of the farm labourers were governed by the seasons: mulled ale drunk in the cold winter and sweet mead consumed at harvest time when the warm sun turned the corn a golden yellow.

Hartshill: only one thing betters this view

All this has changed, with central heating ensuring an even temperature throughout the year. To most people the Noahs Ark, is just somewhere to call into after a visit to the hospital or a meeting place to discuss the day's work. It is said that the presence of some of the founder members of the community can still be felt in many older buildings, but if you see or hear something unexplainable, don't be afraid of the ghosts of the past. Everyone who has had a home as solid as those in Hartshill finds it hard to settle anywhere else and the land around the Noahs Ark is clearly too good to leave.

KIDSGROVE

THE PLOUGH INN

Looking through the windows of the Plough Inn on a warm summer evening, it is difficult to see beyond the houses of today. Are there any indications left of some of the previous occupants of Kidsgrove? Many will think not, nevertheless the smells, sights and sounds are there if time is given to discover them.

The first people to find the high ground ideal for habitation were probably warriors in the pre-Saxon times looking for new land to conquer. Although quite bleak the area between the cliffs on which the Ravens roosted and the wooded area where their Rookeries were was high enough to afford a little protection from the marauding Celts. Perhaps these were the first people to call the Kidsgrove area their home. They brought customs and the Latin language, native to most of the invaders to these shores, and words and habits picked up from the settlements they passed on their travels. The encampments they built beside the river Trent formed the first small villages of Staffordshire. When the families of these first settlers grew too big the strong young men of the family moved further inland. When leaving the family home these younger members took with them gifts from the family to start a new settlement. Animal skins to make shelters, rope to secure the fences, salt to flavour the food, and cooking pots. The elders always kept these pots filled with a residue made from boiling leaves and roots gathered from the countryside, believing that this would mean that the new village would never go hungry.

It is possible that a young warrior chief found the area sheltered enough from the cold winds but still affording a clear view of approaching enemies to begin a new settlement. The first task was to send his scouts out to find water, probably from the area around the Brieryhurst. Sticks from Hardings Wood would be gathered to build fires, to protect his men from the wild animals that still abounded in the Clough area and to warm them against the cold winds that blew across the open land to the north. Here, he set his pot down and began to cook his first meal.

When asked by the few natives what was in the pots, the warriors would say "Lubbe" or "Loopie" – which was their way of describing the natives who they considered clumsy and stupid – and "Salio" meaning salt water or sauce. Gradually the word 'Lobscouse' became a way to describe the concoction which formed a major part of the diet of the new settlers. This food, along with many of the invaders' customs, became part of the area's history.

Most of this was long forgotten until the 'navigators', under the orders of that great engineer James Brindley, began the task of carving a waterway from the river Mersey to the Trent. These men were considered alien to the local people who lived in the villages and were not allowed to live too close to them. The *Navvies* as they were called had worked their way along the newly formed Canal from Liverpool and they, like the warriors before, spoke a different dialect – making it even harder for them to integrate. The townspeople made these rough men pitch their tents just outside the main villages, with most of the food they ate being gathered from the countryside and cooked on open fires. Often these men would be escorted out of the Ale houses of the villages because of their behaviour which was often no more troublesome than the locals. These men missed their homes by the sea, missed the foods that they were used to and most of all missed their own dialect.

Kidsgrove continued to develop as a mining village with several collieries. Plans for a great tunnel to service this burgeoning industry were unveiled by Brindley. It was driven through Harecastle Hill and became known as Harecastle Tunnel. According to the tunnel keeper and local tradition, the ambitious plan was ridiculed as 'a castle in the air' – being yet another derivation of 'Harecastle'. It is 2897 yards long and 8 feet 6 inches wide. It took 6 years to build and Brindley died before its completion, leaving his brother-in-law, Henshall to finish the task. The Harecastle Hotel got is name from the tunnel and there is another association – the Kidsgrove Boggart. This is the ghost of a woman who was murdered in the tunnel. She appears minus hear head, shrieking and crying to warn of impending disasters in the local mines.

The navvies who dug the tunnel were slowly accepted by some of the locals. Friendships built up between the men and some of the local girls. Marriages took place, a few at the local Church near the tunnel entrance, and this brought about a new group of people that spoke a mixture of the North Midlands dialect and the earthy tones that come from many generations by the sea ports.

Food was an important part of the immigrant's life. The stew that the warriors in pre-Saxon times had called Lobscouse was something that both the navvies and the local people knew well, and this became the staple diet of most of the people who lived and worked by the canal. The stew that those first inhabitants to the area had called Lobscouse the navvies from Liverpool had for many years called Scouse, while the local people chose the first part of the word. Gradually, other ingredients were added as the finances of the people began to flourish. The concoction that started life all those years ago as a gift to ensure good fortunes had become a dish that is synonymous with The Potteries.

Perhaps some of the workers from the modern Hardingswood Industrial Estate who call in to The Plough Inn on their way home from work have more in common with those first workers than the many family names that can be traced back to the Navvies. The sounds and smells that drifts along Ravenscliff Road are probably a mixture of friendly words of greeting, good quality beer and that smell that has meant home since as far back as the history of the area. Lobby is as good now as it was to those first settlers who called Kidsgrove home.

Harecastle Tunnel

LONGPORT

THE PACKHORSE

Echoes of the past are all around that wonderful drinking place, The Packhorse. The sounds of tired feet against stone changed only slightly over the years. The whistling of workmen can still be heard as they walk along Station Road – though the songs are different from those of Gertie Gitana, the darling of the Music Hall, who was born in Longport in 1888. The occasional sound of a motor stopping is more likely to be that of a car on the car park than a great barge coming to a halt at the wharf, but with eyes closed and a little imagination it is possible to travel back to the days before container lorries took goods to far-off places. Although Longport (or Longbridge) and The Pack Horse Inn existed before the Trent and Mersey Canal was opened in the mid 1700s, it was not until then that the gradual process of industrialisation began to change the once-rural communities.

As the 1800s began, bottle ovens and huddles of low buildings hugged the water's edge at Longport. They initially gave the area the appearance of a shanty town. One of the most famous local factories was Price and Kensington, making the world-famous Price's National Tea Pots or as many local people call them affectionately "Brown Bettys". These large round vessels bring back memories of social occasions before bar meals were available in local pubs.

In streets throughout the area,pinafored ladies had large kettles and Brown Betties complete with long-handled spoons – which would appear when a family gathered to mark an important occasion. When the first visitor arrived, endless cups of tea began to appear from the small scullery with best china for the immediate family then plain blue cups and saucers for the lesser members and children. Plates of muffins would be set out in the parlour, with fruit bread for funerals and best boiled ham for weddings. It was left to a small band of trainee helpers, with a hat to suit the occasion firmly secured with a hat pin, to return each item of clean crockery and the dark wood dining chairs to their own home. Only the menfolk would have time take a breath of air which often ended with a slow walk to the pub.

The factories of Longport and throughout the area gave work to many people. All workers were proud of their own trade, and each tradesperson in the pottery industry had a title that brought amusement to people who lived beyond the smoky atmosphere. The 'throwers' and 'placers' were quite understandable, but what of the blungers, fettlers, jolliers, jigger workers – and the profession that brings the biggest smile: sagger maker's bottom knocker. This was a skilled tradesman who worked with the sagger maker who made the fire clay boxes which protected the ware from the flames. The bottom knocker's job was to use a wooden mallet called a mawl or mow to knock a lump of clay into shape inside an iron hoop. This was attached to a sheet of clay which had previously been wrapped around a wooden drum to give it its shape. A flat piece of wood was rubbed over the joins to seal them, and the resulting 'saggar' was fired at a high temperature. The 'green' or unfired ware was placed in the saggar and returned to the oven for firing.

This process, along with many others, has changed. But the wharf that once bustled with dust-covered barges has found a new use. Pleasure boats are now to be seen at Longport, though many owners of these craft rarely give the area a second glance. But the Pack Horse is still a popular place with both visitors and locals.

Longport: low buildings that once hummed with life

LONGTON: LANE END

THE ALBION

There once were many public houses between Calverley Street and Chadwick Street (known locally as High Street Lane End but actually Uttoxeter Road, Longton). Of the few that remain, The Albion is one of those that has changed least. It has small shining windows and several original features, including a friendly ghost. The Albion has always given a special welcome to Pot Bank workers calling in after a hard day's work at the factory. Today's customers are very different from the ragged workers who trudged the cobbled streets when The Albion was in its infancy.

The Albion : always a special welcome to pot bank workers

ragged workers who trudged the cobbled streets when The Albion was in its infancy.

Although James Turner was one of the first potters to use the clay in the 1750s, little thought was given to the living conditions of the workers. Gradually, other potters began to buy land around the ancient Roman Road between Newcastle and Derby. When this, along with other roads, was turnpiked in 1759 it opened up the area, with carters taking ware to be sold at the markets in the surrounding towns.

Thomas and Michael Shelley bought a site between the Leigh Street and Chadwick Street area in 1787 and began a tradition that was to take the name of Longton all over the world. Bottle ovens of all shapes appeared and little workshops coloured the landscape. By the mid 1800s the Pottery industry was breathing life into Longton, but what breath! The air around The Albion public house whose licensee, according to Kelly's Directory of 1840 was a J. Bladon, was filled with the stench of smoke from the chimneys and bad drainage. Potters like Richard Hodson, whose factory was a three storied building with a fine facade overlooking the main road, gave little thought to the people who came from all over the country looking for work. Warrens of small dwellings were tucked away in the area between Normacot Road and Sutherland Road. Cobbled streets and back-to-back houses were built in areas that were once completely rural.

Tiny dwellings were packed around communal yards that housed a wash house, privy and ash pit. Short Street still contains some of the remaining few houses left as a reminder of that dreadful time. Most of the others have been obliterated as if to eliminate their existence.

This area supplied many workers for George Proctor's factory site which he took over in 1881. The two-roomed houses were sometimes occupied by a dozen or more people working long hours in poor conditions, with little time to notice their deprivations. Young children were expected to work a twelve-hour shift at the factory for very little pay. With money scarce, young and old had little more than a bowl of stodgy oatmeal gruel to start the day. Perhaps with this in mind and a little imagination the following tale can be visualised.

"One cold rainy morning, before dawn, a small boy is woken by his uncle, home from the night shift at the factory eager to crawl into the boys warm bed. Bleary eyed the boy dresses for his shift at the local pot bank. With no bread to take the boy tucks a scrap of stale cheese into his pocket, too late for breakfast his mother arms him with a bowl of gruel to eat later.

Still dark and raining hard, the lad trudges through the back entries of Chelson Street. Quickening his steps as he crosses the graveyard of St James Church, past the Albion pub still smelling strongly of last night's drinking session, he goes into the comparative warmth of the factory. A glowing kiln already casts an amber glow around the yard. The kilnsman is busily attending to the firemouth – and cooking himself a slice of bacon on his shovel before the boss arrives. Taking pity on the poor wretch but with only enough bacon for one, the old man scoops a spoonful of the now watered-down gruel onto the hot shovel. After a while, the pancake was taken out of the fire and the cheese added; this was rolled up and eaten while still hot, thereby making a tasty meal for the lad and kilnman, with the smell bringing the apprentice kilnsman along to join the feast. The cooking of pancakes on the fire shovel became a regular occurrence at the factory, with throwers, dippers and casters all coming out of their workshops to the kilnsman for their pancakes.

When the kilnsman was too infirm to continue the heavy work, but still needing money to keep his family, he carried on making the pancakes in the parlour of his home, on a griddle instead of his kilnsman's shovel. He refined the mixture until it was a smooth oatmeal batter and sold them to the local people on their way to work. The oatcake shop was born. Slowly the oatcake became the staple diet for the pottery worker, making the morning more bearable.

Although it would be impossible to verify the facts this is quite plausible and makes for a good tale.

Traders began to see the potential of the new houses and factories in High Street, Lane End and started to open small shops along the road opposite St James Church, and among the factories. Grocers, animal food shops, small drapers and even sweet shops all became busy selling some of the goods needed by the people

While George Procter was taking over Gladstone Works in the late 1800s, Edward Joseph Walker began to make a rather delicious toffee for his special customers; everyone who came into the sweet-shop began to comment on the toffee and his business boomed. By the time his son took over in 1915, they were producing toffee made only with full cream milk, the finest butter and sugar at a factory site near the shop. Children who sat in the doorway of the Albion waiting for their fathers must have felt quite a craving as the sweet smell of Walker's toffe wafted over them.

Walkers Nonsuch Toffee was named after the famous palace built by Henry VIII and its fame spread across the country. A bigger site was needed and a factory in Calvary Street was chosen to continue the fine reputation set up in the late 1800s.

The Gladstone factory carried on trading, with the Albion becoming a popular meeting place for the workers. The Vulcan public house was connected to the factory, but the Albion was said to have better beer on tap. The fortunes of the pottery industry have always fluctuated and at one time in the 1930s, there was Doctor Chadwick's surgery, Evans the undertaker, and a private house all on the factory site.

By the 1960s the fortunes had run out and the site was derelict with the more efficient gas-fired tunnels replacing the old kilns. But preservation orders have been placed on many buildings that were once regarded as slums. With help, this heritage will never be forgotten. Although many individual factories have been taken over, the traditions and skills of the Lane End people will always be remembered and pot bank workers will hopefully enjoy the hospitality of the Albion public house for many years to come.

LONGTON

THE SHAMROCK INN

The sound of beer being delivered in high pressured metal kegs hardly brings the locals and visitors to the windows of the Shamrock Public House. As the dray men drive away, those who have ventured from their warm seats and cool beer can look out on to open plan gardens and neat houses though, until recently, the area around this side of Heathcote Road seemed to be just a remnant of a time long gone. It is only a three minute walk from the busy market, with its mock Victorian design, selling everything from fresh fish to computer games.

Longton Market

The area around Gold Street and the pub is more in keeping with a time when there were more public houses in Longton than shops, with most of the inhabitants having their homes in the passageways that filled the outskirts of the town. These poor people had little time to notice the architecture of their surroundings, and what spare time they did have was filled with ways of earning a few extra pennies. The sound of a beer delivery would bring them out onto the cobbled streets with the hope of giving the drayman a hand as he steadied his horse in exchange for the price of a pint, or with bucket and shovel in hand they would follow the cart. But these were not the first inhabitants of Longton to earn money for the little extras in life.

The winding road that led from Blurton, is now filled with groups of houses that span the building techniques of builders over the years. From small cottages that seem to call out for the thatcher's knife to modern semis with satellite dishes. Once this area was completely rural, with fresh water streams turning primitive mills to grind corn, quiet nooks to hide in while out hunting and undulating meadows ideal for the rich land owners to build their homes on.

One such land-owner of the Longton Hall estate was Sir John Edensor Heathcote, who through birthright and marriage was descended from a rich Derbyshire family. With his careful management the estate flourished and gave work to many young people who had been driven out of the textile towns of the north through poverty and deprivation. These workers who probably lived in lean-to shacks on the estate became the envy of others on the bordering farms, as Longton Hall workers had the protection of the Great Hall.

Gradually small groups of family cottages began to grow, each group clustered around the bends of that winding road giving the area its individual shape. Each group was known by a local name, some of which have been lost, while others remain even today.

By the mid-1700s, the pottery and coal industries were beginning to form. In the main towns of the northern parts of Stoke-on-Trent, clay and coal were being dug out of the ground at an ever increasing rate to produce a living for the people. The clay found by John Turner on the Longton Hall estate was far superior to that which he was working with at his factory in Stoke. With a few locals he set up a small factory on the land between what is now known as Edensor and the area known by locals as Green Dock. Here he produced a high standard of stoneware that was to give the name of Longton world-wide fame.

Turner died quite young and his final resting place was at Brewood Hall, Wolverhampton. The factory bearing his name closed in the early

1800s, but his influence in the forming of Longton will never be forgotten.

Gradually the farmland that the gentry were so proud of became scarred with the industrial revolution. The streams were so polluted that Longton Hall became uninhabitable and was allowed to fall into disrepair. Great marl holes appearing where once animals grazed.

Those who had chosen to live within the bounds of the smoke-belching chimneys gave the town a population of hard working, but poorly paid people. Their poverty unknown to the farm workers of years before gave the people an eagerness to earn money in many ways.

Old men repaired shoes in the front rooms of the terraced houses and some sold hot roast potatoes on cold days outside the Town Hall. Children gathered sticks and outcropped coal to be sold on the street corners of Stafford

Longton Pot Bank

Street (now renamed The Strand). Young men would be seen entering the Shamrock Public House in long coats with copious pockets that would hold anything from rabbits, hares and wood pigeon to mushrooms and watercress gathered early in the morning from the few remaining areas of wooded land by the brooks. These would be sold to anyone with a few coppers to spare.

Rabbit Stew and Jugged Hare made a welcome supplement to the monotonous but wholesome diet of Lobby.

With a great many new delicacies to wet the appetites of workers as they walk along The Strand and friendly butchers to supply fresh meat, there is little need nowadays for the poachers who frequented the Shamrock. But even today there are still a few regulars who can, for a small consideration, produce a fresh skinned rabbit for a special friend. Today's locals are not as poor as those of the last century, but there are still many hard working people around The Shamrock.

MEIR

THE KING'S ARMS

As one of the few great buildings left standing in the Meir, The King's Arms public house overlooks an area that has seen more changes than many. The original centre of the community has almost disappeare and the Meir that our ancestors knew remains only as a fond memory.

Like most places Meir began its life as just a crossing, with the Roman Legionaries probably the first visitors to discover the inhospitable water-logged ground. These Latin-speakers called the area "Crux-o-Mere" which broadly translates to 'the crossing over the sea or water'. The area gradually became, after the passing of time and the coming of the Anglo Saxons, a track, best to be avoided if possible. After the Romans left the area in approximately 200 AD, many of their roads were allowed to fall into disrepair.

The people who were left behind called the track that crossed from the fort outside the present town of Newcastle to the fortifications at Stone, "Mere". This translates to 'separated' or 'unmixed', probably because the natives in the area were slightly different from the people who lived in the larger settlements. Out of this grew the word "Meare" meaning boundary, which is how most people of that time saw any area that stood on the edge of what they considered civilisation.

At this time much of the area around Staffordshire was beginning to be subdivided into parcels of land owned by the better educated people. Two areas had their borders at approximately where the centre of The Meir now stands. The Totmonslow Hundred and the Pirehill Hundred both met at the place then called "meare". This coincides well with the name by the previous residents and gives another dimension in the naming of the community.

Many people wonder why locals call the area "The Meir". Meir has its origins steeped in a time long before ordinary people could read and write, describing where they lived in a language a lot less complex than that which we use today. After the Romans left the area to colonise other parts of Britain this language slowly began to form. "Crux-o-Mere" became "The Mere Crossing". With the passing of time and quite a few variations along the way the area became known as "the Crossing at The

Meare". With the need we all have to save words when we speak, it has become known to all as "The Meir".

By the 1600s, a small group of dwellings was built on the higher ground and, although the crossing was waterlogged, it was still used as the main track between the trading towns of Newcastle and Derby. The enterprising people of Meir charged a small toll for escorting the wealthy merchants over the waterlogged ground at Meir, with an extra charge for carrying the merchant over.

At about this time, a small farm house stood at the site of the present Kings Arms and, as well as producing food for the family, the farmer's wife would brew beer and bake bread to sell to the passing travellers. The reputation of this farm and ale house at the crossing had spread, with people gradually making it into a staging post between the larger villages of Cheadle and Stoke.

Possibly this how the settlement would have remained if it was not for the fact that the Civil War of 1643 brought soldiers and horses through the crossing. Their combined weight made the rough track into a fairly noticeable road.

The turnpiking of the Newcastle to Uttoxeter road in 1771 brought more dramatic changes to the Meir with a toll gate across the road. The toll house stood at approximately where Pickford Place now stands, but it was the Ale House that stood at the crossing that saw to the needs of most of the travellers.

The Meir began to form into a small community with a public house, cattle dealer and a few farms scattered about the crossing. Until the late 1880s, the Meir was still in the Parish of Caverswall, but a new church was built on the high ground near the crossroads. People appreciated the beauty of Holy Trinity Church with its elevated position; the ringing of the bell called people from all around to enter its grand doors. William Havergal Brian was employed as organist at the age of 14 in the early 1900s, and went on to become a renowned composer. Perhaps this church has always been slightly over-shadowed by St. James' Church, just down the road, and the Saxon church of St. Peter's at Caverswall. When Reginald Mitchell, the designer of the world-famous Spitfire aeroplane, was married to local dairy farmer's daughter Florence Dyson, Holy Trinity merited only a few lines in a letter he sent to his brother. Nevertheless, it has grown like the community, to what it is now: a thriving church full of interesting people.

As the 20th century progressed, so did the need for better facilities in the Meir. Although many small towns were lucky enough to have theatres that could also be used as cinemas, a purpose-built cinema was erected here. Regrettably, the Broadway, along with many other cinemas, has long-since gone.

The Broadway

Its formal opening was in 1936 and it finally closed its glass-panelled doors in 1971. Almost every person over the age of 30 within a bus ride of the Meir has their own tale to tell about the Broadway. Even from those far off days when Arthur Tracey captivated the hearts of the nation with his handsome looks and perfect manners, the most popular words on young people's lips were "Meet me at the Broadway". The double seats at the back ensured that nothing came between the embraces of true love, and only the watchful eye of Mr. Plumton and the glow from the torch of the blond usherette ensured that nobody came into the cinema via the green fire doors.

The 1950s brought new thrills to the people of the Meir. Television and coffee bars brought a new type of customer to the Kings Arms public house, which had to entertain teddy boys trying to emulate the anti- hero of the day, James Dean. Many parked their high-powered bikes on the forecourt of the pub much to the annoyance of the people who would like nothing better than a quiet stroll along Weston Road on a warm summer's evening.

The Meir that the traveller sees today as he speeds along the A50 says little of the varied past that has given the area its heritage. Even the older people who use the modern facilities that the Adult and Community Centre provides can only remember a little of the past. Perhaps one day the Meir will be lost in that sea of modern roads and concrete with only the Church and The Kings Arms left to remind people of the old Meir. However one thing is certain, the name bestowed on this compact area will survive, remembered as a place where The Kings Arms has always stood, calling out a welcome out to all who pass.

The King's Arms – always offering a welcome

NEWCASTLE-UNDER-LYME

THE SLUG AND LETTUCE

Each of the public houses in Newcastle has a name that gives it a personality of its own. But one stands out more than all the others, not just for the excellent food and drink served there, but for a name that is so individual as to bring a smile of recognition to people's faces. This name goes back much further than Newcastle itself and makes claim to a time even before some of the oldest pubs in the area.

The Slug and Lettuce: a sign to bring a smile to your face

Long ago, when peoples drinking habits were governed by their social position, the interior of the taverns or ale houses were divided by partitions. Some were solid walls, while others were open trellis built to let the upper class peer at the working man – considered by the business people to be quite an enjoyable pastime. The ale-houses were talked about, with the trellis or lattice windows being an important point when deciding where to spend the evening. Very soon some pubs were known by the type of partition or 'lattice' they had. The word changed with the passing of time to lettuce, the slug part of the name was probably added as a joke by some locals (the interiors of the first drinking places were not as clean as they could have been) and then it stuck – giving a title that would be remembered long after the architecture of the drinking places had changed. Even if wasn't exactly the way The Slug and Lettuce gained its name, this tale makes for a good ice-breaker at the many get-togethers in the now elegant rooms of the solid looking pub that looks across to the bus station.

Newcastle, along with many other towns was starting to grow by the Middle Ages and social drinking gave man a way to relax and spend time with good friends. But this was not the only thing the working man did in the ale-houses, smoking was beginning to grow in popularity towards the turn of the 16th century.

The first people to smoke pipes were not, as many people think today, old ladies in their rocking chairs outside the front doors of the terraced houses. Towns like Newcastle had streets with names reminiscent of the great tobacco manufacturers. Roads like Holborn Road, where one old lady sat smoking a penn'orth of twist from a long Church Warden's pipe on a summer evening before it was decided to be unfashionable.

The habit of inhaling smoke was already widespread in the New World by the time Sir Walter Raleigh had brought back the leaves of the tobacco plant to Queen Elizabeth I. The monks and priests in the temples and the tribal Chiefs of North America were inhaling hemp and opium from ceremonial pipes to induce an intoxicating stupor, thereby achiev-ing a closer link with the spirit world long before social smoking became accepted. Consequently it can be understood why pipes were never invented – they just grew out of the need man has always had to be at peace with the world.

Cornish Fishermen were removing the flesh from the narrow end of huge crabs' claws to produce primitive pipes at the same time as the Monbutto Natives who lived on the Congo centuries ago had discovered how to make a pipe from a plantation leaf.

Clay pipes were produced as early as 1575 in Shropshire when pipe smoking was in its infancy in England.

By the 1600s, Newcastle was one of the major producers of clay pipes in England. The clay that was just under the ground in the area between

Shelton and Hanley proved ideal for pipes. Dr Plott, when writing about the area in the 1700s, spoke of the whitish blue clay that burnt full and white and of the pipe makers of North Staffordshire. Of the many manufactures at this time, some of whom produced clay pipes as a side line to their major work, Charles Riggs was probably one of the most famous.

Victorian socialites met in the many public houses that abounded in the cities and towns in the 1800s and smoking was encouraged. A social grace of that time was the hiring of pipes from the bar of the ale house, with the smoker paying one penny and the landlord trusting him to take no more than one fill of his pipe from the ornate jar. Smoking has come a long way since then, with one of the last pipe manufactures in the area registered as Eccles of Higherland closing its doors at the beginning of the 1900s.

People today prefer the smell of something sweeter than the strong black twist that was shredded and packed in to the fragile clay pipes. Perhaps even the most expensive Mechum pipes made from Solidified Sea Foam do not give as much pleasure as the tuppenny pipes that were smoked by men and women of long ago.

The Newcastle that the busy commuter sees is very different from the town the old umbrella maker would see as he sat on his wooden chair behind St. Giles Church over 50 years ago. Not only were there sturdy umbrellas to be repaired and sold to the gents of the town, but also delicate lace trimmed umbrellas for elegant ladies to carry as they walked along the Brampton for a Sunday afternoon stroll.

Memories and tales persist – like that of the local lady who, when interviewed in 1926 about her longevity, spoke of the pleasure she gained from smoking over three ounces of tobacco a week in her favourite churchwarden pipe which she had smoked since a young girl in her pinafore. The occasional bowl of a clay pipe can still be discovered when the never-ending building work is carried out to transform the once tiny market town into just one more shopping complex.

These are all that are left of the Newcastle known to our Grandfathers, but hopefully people will carry on talking long into the future about a part of the history of Newcastle that has been somewhat neglected.

NORMACOT

THE NORMACOT HOTEL

What a monument to the builders of the 1930s The Normacot Hotel is: standing grand and solid like some ancient Hall, walled in as if to protect it from the marauding people.

The Normacot Hotel

Nothing could be further from the truth, the low walls and solid doors are there to welcome people who have ventured off the busy A50. To many people, this red-brick building with its tall chimneys, airy rooms and fancy windows seems out of place. There seems nothing but open spaces and endless short roads around; only occasionally does a complete row of neat terraced houses break the monotonous view.

Why then did such a monument to man's favourite pastime get rebuilt when the original Normacot Public House, a tiny place further down the road, would have been quite adequate for the few people who live in Normacot? Well, the fact is that Normacot has not always been bleak; it was once a busy community with its boundaries stretching way beyond the present ones. It has a rich history that goes back far beyond its neighbouring communities of Meir and Longton, even before the first potters began to use the clay in the surrounding area.

The name of the area itself says something of its former inhabitants, descendants of fierce warriors who had used the rivers as highways began to travel inland looking for new settlement area long before the Domesday Survey was started.

These Norsemen built small huts or cots on the sheltered ground, probably near the brooks that watered the area. Gradually the Norsemen-cots began to grow, with mills to grind corn, farm buildings and fertile ground giving food to the animals that had become the major part of the economy of the area.

When the industrial revolution began to alter this first community, rows of terraced houses began to appear, mostly built under the direction of the local pottery manufacturers. All of the land around here was part of the Duke of Sutherland's enormous estate. They decided that Normacot was just far enough away from the smoky chimneys to provide slightly healthier living conditions for workers.

Gradually a few of these pottery manufacturers began to realise that workers needed more than houses. The Ale Houses that at first were only front rooms began to improve and it was decided to build a cinema. That wonderful building The Alhambra saw many grand stars, both on screen and making personal appearances before it closed its doors in the late 1970s.

The young families that lived in roads with names forever linking them with the Duke of Sutherland's estate in Scotland, names like Argyll, Athol, Rothesay all needed educating and schools were built. The first were church schools, then came that wonderful sprawling school, Queensbury Road, with high walls segregating the boys from the girls. Large classrooms heated with coal fires and wooden desks and forms with metal frames to catch cold fingers on. Each desk had its own inkwell and a groove for a split-nib pen.

One of the most famous pupils of the school was the son of Mr Mitchell the local schoolmaster, a small boy who lived in a larger than average terraced house, off Belgrave Road. He played in the yards and gardens of Normacot, fascinated by the new inventions that were being put into use daily. He was to grow up to become world-famous for ideas that were formed in those classrooms. Although not his birthplace Reginald Mitchell will always be remembered as spending his formative years in Normacot. The education and encouragement he gained from his teachers and parents would make his design for the Spitfire Airplane world famous.

Along with schools in the area small shops began to open to supply the goods needed for the ever growing population. These shops covered both sides of the main road as well as many corners of the smaller roads. Without these corner shops Normacot might never have survived.

The staple diet of people in the early 1900s was bread. Not the pre-packed bleached tasteless stuff on sale in supermarkets today but small loaves with friendly names such as cottage, bloomers, tin loaves and cobs. The aroma from Bengry's Bakery would drift across the roof tops every morning, somehow mixing with the other smells of beer brewing and coal fires burning to give a warm welcome to the coldest of mornings. Most of the shops in Normacot would open their doors before dawn to ensure the bread delivery was attended to long before the first customer appeared.

However, bread was not the only thing these shops would sell. A good corner shop, and Normacot had quite a few, would sell everything from saucepans to pins. The shelves that covered the walls of the shops in upper Normacot Road and Chaplin Road would be piled high with Nestles Condensed Milk, Colman's Mustard and Tate and Lyle Black Treacle. While the bacon slicer and shiny brass scales stood on the counter eagerly waiting for a customer with a straw basket over her arm to decide how much middle bacon was required. On the sawdust-covered floor stood sacks of tea, sugar and flour, alongside carrots, potatoes and turnips.

Little thought was given to hygiene, and illness was commonplace all over the city, but Normacot was lucky to have a small hospital that opened in 1890. Although primitive by today's standards, it began the tradition of care and attention that is still carried on today.

By the time the new Normacot Hotel had been built, Normacot was already feeling the strain of the bigger towns pulling people away from its heart. With only the barest of buildings remaining intact, perhaps one day new life will come to the area. Until then, the Normacot Hotel must remain what it has been since it first opened its doors: a great place to feel safe in and enjoy a pint of good quality beer.

NORTON

THE ROBIN HOOD

The road between Leek and Endon is filled with villages that seem somehow to run into each other with borders that are hard to define. One thing that is certain though, once away from the industrial towns that for many centuries have produced the goods that gave the area its name, the landscape gets more rugged and the winds get colder. Places where shelter can be found became a necessity the further north you get. Perhaps this is why the Robin Hood Public House has become so popular with visitors since it first opened its doors. The warm smell of its extra friendly rooms seem somehow to waft across Ford Green Road and beckon people in.

Since a time before motorways and fast cars linked the Pottery towns with the textile towns of the north and modern pubs filled the country-side of North Staffordshire this road has been used by men for trading and living.

When William had the Doomsday Survey compiled, Nortone (Norton) was noted as being valued at 40 shillings, this made it quite an asset for Robert of Stafford who owned it. The area then consisted of two hides of land, four ploughs, a wood three Leagues long and two Leagues wide.

Small groups of shelters were huddled together at this time against the cold winds and the constant threat of marauding villains who gained their living by wandering the countryside sacking defenceless villages and terrorising the people. These outlaws were feared by the peace-loving people around Norton and only the very brave elders of the village ventured beyond the wooden stockade that surrounded the village.

Not all outlaws were feared though, some by' the mid-1300s were looked on as heroes. Tales were beginning to be told by travellers as they sat around the fires in the shelters of Norton drinking home-brewed ale and sharing a meal with the people of the village. Great deeds of bravery were told, especially of one band of men whose names began to become synonymous with the protection of the underdog.

The brave leader of this band of men was, according to official records in Barnsdale, born in Wakefield in 1285. He was the son of a local forester who was banished after the defeat of Edward II, to the forests that covered most of Nottingham and the borders of Staffordshire. The friends who followed him were all like-minded people who fought against the tyranny of the corrupt clergy and officials of the time. This man and his followers who lived like ruffians depended on the generosity of the poor people when food was scarce. However, when food was plentiful, the feasts in the forests were shared by many.

Their adventures would help to relieve the monotony and children would often relive the battles that were fought around the great castle at Nottingham in the encampment at the village of Norton.

Many centuries have passed since the leader of the band was laid to rest beneath an oak tree where he had fired his final arrow, just 500 yards from the river Calder. His death bed was in a small room at Kirklees Abbey farm near Huddersfield with his beloved wife Marion by his side. His memory lives on for ever in stories, songs and films. What better name to give a place where good company can be found and nourishing refreshments obtained than ''The Robin Hood''. The naming of this public house was still far into the future when the Rev. Richard Malkin tried to instill some religion into the people of Norton in the 1500s. This was difficult when most farms brewed some form of alcohol.

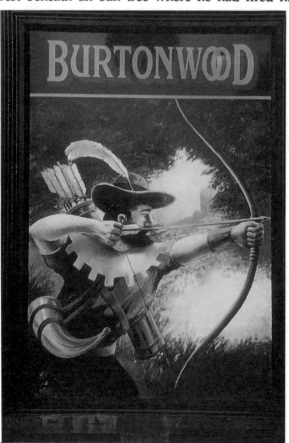

The settlement of Norton was of sufficient size at this time to warrant an entry in Yates' map, although it was not as large as its neighbouring village Endon.

The mines that first gave employment to many local people began to bring new life into the area, with rows of houses filling the area with sounds and smells that were unknown to the first settlers.

One of the more notable sons of Norton was Robert Heath, who progressed from a wage of 5 shillings a week to being a millionaire owning several coal and ironstone mines and iron works, and the largest employer of labour in North Staffordshire. When his son reached the age of 21, in 1868, he granted a holiday with pay to all his workers. In the grounds of nearby Ford Green Hall, an enormous marquee was erected that supplied food that even the best party nights at the Robin Hood would be proud of. The list of the feast left people speechless: the fare included 6000 lbs of meat, 800 loaves of bread, 4000 plum puddings, 2340 gallons of ale, 2300 bottles of ginger beer, 4000 papers of tobacco, 400 bottles of claret, 100 bottles of champagne, 100 lbs of fish (including salmon).

Only a few old areas remain. The occasional farm still stands to give an idea of what Norton was like when the canal men and the coal hauliers would argue about the price of transporting of coal along the nearby Cauldon Canal.

Nevertheless, Norton will remain one of the outpost villages that has given North Staffordshire its individual shape. The Robin Hood public house remains a place were people can enjoy the hospitality of the area long into the future.

PENKHULL

THE GREYHOUND

With many reminders of its former life as a court and lock up, the Greyhound public house seems somehow to pass judgment on the village. With a little careful investigation, some evidence of the past can be revealed. Solid doors and tiny windows tend to give an authoritarian look, but once inside all this changes: shining bars, sparkling glasses and friendly staff are only too eager to serve customers, with a courtesy unknown to the Court House staff many years ago. However Penkhull has always had a way of dealing with felons that goes back much further than when the Court first sat in session at the Greyhound.

The Greyhound: small windows overlook the village

Celtic warriors were probably the first settlers on the hill by the edge of the wooded area. Evidence of their presence is revealed in the settlement's name *Pencet* which was the Celtic word for 'pointed end' and *hyll* meaning 'high'.

These people seemed little more than savages, and they dealt with their enemies in a quick and drastic way. Marauding renegades who had ventured beyond their own settlements were put to the sword as soon as they were seen venturing up the hill.

At the beginning of the 1200s, the Saxon Earl of Algar owned the settlement and inhabitants of Pencethyl, with the Domesday survey recording Penchetel having 17 villeins or the lowest class of serfs, six borders and eight ploughs, with a wooded area of one league long and eight furlongs wide. Compared to the neighbouring village of Stoke, it made it quite a busy settlement.

King John had begun to deforest the area by 1204 and the township of Penchyll became part of the great manor of Newcastle-under-Lyme with violence being an everyday occurrence. Although that foundation stone of human liberty The Magna Carta was signed by the reluctant King in 1215, it took many months for its effects to be felt in the village square. However, gradually the feudal system of life was beginning to change, giving the people an opportunity to own and work their own land as well as for the Lord of the Manor. A small mill on the settlement was used to grind corn and fish ponds provided fresh fish for the landowner.

Crime figures in the Middle Ages would tax even the resources of any modern police force. The landowners way of dealing with felons had altered very little over the centuries, with hangings being common-place and legal quarrels dealt with by ordeal of combat.

Gradually people began to condemn this old method of punishment. A new way began to filter through from the Court of Henry II who issued a decree known as the "Assize of Clarendon". This new method of trial by jury seemed very strange to the people of Penchall who had always lived in complete obeisance to the Lord of the Manor and the Church at Stoke. The system gave the responsibility of finding out the truth to "twelve free and law abiding men". Although slightly fairer, it took many years to eliminate all the defects to give us the roots of the English legal system that we use today.

Some of the King's men at the castle at Newcastle had the job of looking after the stables. These custodians of the stables were then given the responsibility of escorting felons to the lock-up at Penchall that had been erected in 1355. As the population increased so did the constables' job and other lock-ups had to be constructed in nearby villages.

The Penchall of 1600 included the open fields of Stubbs, Oldfield, Woodfield, Churchfields and Cherryfield, all of which have now been swallowed up by the sprawling estates of Stoke, Hartshill and Newcastle.

Quarrying began on the land around Penchall in the early 1800s and most of the men who worked the stone, some of which was used to repair the nearby Stoke Bridge, were hard and brutal. There were regular fights in the square over everything from the ownership of livestock, to robbery, and spells in the lock-up were a regular part of their life. Daily reminders of these days can be seen by anyone who passes Quarry Road and Quarry Avenue.

Poverty was another cause of crime. To try to combat this, a workhouse was built in 1735 for the parish of Stoke at the southern end of Penkall at the junction of Penkall Green and the road to Trentham, which provided a refuge for the destitute.

Farming land covered much of the area. In 1760 Grindley Hill farm and house stood on the north side of Penchall in London Road. It provided a little of the fresh food for the governors of the workhouse, while most of the residents survived on the leftovers.

Gradually, small pottery factories began to alter the landscape. Hugh Booth's Cliff Bank Works stood at the junction of Shelton Old Road and Hartshill Road in the 1780s, trading as Booth and Sons between 1792 and 1837, then trading under various names until it was demolished in 1914. Of the other potters, John Alder's works stood at the junction of Honeywall and what is now Hartshill Road in the early 1800s and produced mottled and tortoiseshell ware. At one time Josiah Wedgwood spent two years with them until he joined Thomas Wheildon in Stoke.

The Chartist Riots in 1842 led to the Chief Bailiffs house at Penkhull being attacked, causing much destruction. Gradually peace was restored and the court sessions became a way of life in the square.

The Reverend Thomas Webb Minton founded the Church of St Thomas the Apostle in the 1800s and will always be remembered in the tablet in the North Aisle of the Church. Although many of the oldest cottages in Penchall are grouped around the Square, most have been altered beyond recognition. Even the Greyhound public house has had many alterations. Part of the original 16th century timbers have been incorporated in the building as it now stands.

According to Kelly's Directory of 1840, among the leading citizens of Penkhull was the licensee of the Greyhound public house and Court, Charles Kirkham. Of the other inhabitants of that time were the parents of Sir Oliver Lodge F.R.S. who was born at The Views, Penkhull in 1851. Sir Oliver was knighted for his pioneering works in electronics in 1902 and died in 1940.

To its neighbour Stoke, Penkhull must now seem quiet and somehow out of place. Perhaps it is taking a justifiable rest after its hard struggle to maintain law and order in the area over the years. However, the Greyhound Public House will hopefully be in the Square at Penkhull for many years to come to keep a watchful eye over the people who enter its doors.

SANDFORD HILL

THE OLD SAL

Although called the "Old Sal", this red brick building standing at the top of a steep hill is a comparatively new drinking place on a modern housing estate. High-tech machines amuse the visitors in open-plan rooms with technology that seems more in fitting to the flight deck of a space station than a public house.

The Old Sal

Those few people who can remember long ago, and can give dates and precise details of the sepia pictures on the wall, remember Sandford Hill when it was only back-entries, yards, school playgrounds and a few open fields with pot banks and pits marking the horizons. All this and many more things make their memories of Sandford Hill people special.

The area around the Old Sal and its brightly-lit rooms is full of memories of the industrial past. The first settlers loved their children and encouraged simple games to teach them to cope with any enemies they would encounter as they grew. The games they played were similar to the Hide and Seek, Rallyo and Ball Tick that children of recent years played around the shops and car park near the pub.

Gradually thatched roofed cottages replaced the first rough shelters on each side of the main track between Adderley Green and the smaller settlements at Longton. Country people of the Middle Ages were poor and most worked on the land as soon as they could reason. Nevertheless the chanting of simple songs would be sung by most children on summer days. 'Ring-a-Ring-of-Roses' is one of the chants that still can be heard in the play area around Clewlow Place and, although the words have lost their original meaning, it is one of the first games that small children learn to play.

Older children have always preferred more boisterous games with a small amount of skill included. By the mid 1800s, the back entries and streets that had been created out of the growing need for accommodation for the many people employed in the pot banks in Longton and the nearby pits of Weston and Mossfield, would be filled with the sounds of metal hoops being beaten with sticks to make them go faster. A few of these hoops came from old beer kegs or barrels from the factories. Most were the wide rims off the 'bone shakers', but this is probably why the game has faded into history, the squat pneumatic tyres of the mountain bike don't have the same hum as the old solid wheeled ones. Other games involved whips which would crack as they were released from the wooden top that spun along the ground, this game was best played on the level ground near St Mary and St Chad Church. Although this involved great concentration as one had to be kept on the top while a look out was always kept for Father Murray in his Biretta and Cassock.

The small school was gradually teaching the children in Sandford Hill the three Rs by the 1900s. But the education gained from games played in the playground of Woodhouse School taught the children much more about life than any lesson scratched on the blackboard with squeaky chalk by a stern faced frock-coated teacher.

Hopscotch was a wonderful game of numbers marked out in back entries with bits of chalk picked up at the end of class or broken moulds brought home from the pot bank by older members of the family.

End terraces provided the ideal spaces for many other games, not just the ball games taught to sibling members of the group by older ones, but what better place to draw cricket stumps or goal posts as well as declarations of true love. Although all this hard work would have to be completely erased with a yard brush and water before the local police-man or the mother of the house found out.

With the coming of gas street-lights in the main streets, new games could be played. A rope turned the post into a thing of pleasure, with children of all ages taking turns to swing the rope. A less adventurous use of a rope was skipping with rhythmic songs that kept the beat with the turn of the rope. Often one end of this rope would be tied to the lamp post if the numbers in the group were small. The mastering of this game would cause much amusement to onlookers as clogged booted boys tried to "Wibble and wobble like a jelly on a plate".

Although ideal for most games, cobbled streets proved disadvantage-ous when marbles were produced from small cloth bags carefully made by loving mothers. "Shotties" with their marvellous colours and desir-able names such as whities and bullies were things to be won, swopped and sometimes even fought over. Getting new ones from the bottle top or again from that wondrous place – the Pot Bank waste tip – was worthy of many a gang meeting.

The two wars brought new words to long established games played around the Albert Street area. The entries where Cowboys and Indians could relive the fights at the O.K. Corral were replaced with soldiers and airmen who would bomb the enemy with great gusto from the tops of the walls. Spies could be captured with the use of the ropes that were once reins for the make-believe horses. Little girls with angelic faces that set out of home on a Saturday morning would have changed before dinner time into tough fighters with as much determination to win as any of Montgomery's men

Perhaps the games played by today's children with flashing lights and complicated rules concern the older people in The Old Sal. But how many of these sensible people were once rough and tumble children who used tin cans for stilts – or 'Winter Warmers', which involved swinging the cans with small amounts of glowing coals. Autumn twi-light evenings would see an orange blur around the open fields where the shops now stand. How many regulars who now play a sedate game of skittles were once cloth-capped boys who would, with a deafening shout at the Royal Cinema, help Buck Rogers save the universe?

Only time will tell what the next generation will remember of their childhood. In Sandford Hill, hopefully their words will be as loving as those that can sometimes be heard today in The Old Sal.

SHELTON

THE BELL AND BEAR

Only the inn sign remains as a reminder

Many travellers who take that long climb from Stoke Station to Howard's Place, Shelton, are looking for a place to unwind. Perhaps with a chance to pit their wits and skills against like minded people.

When they see the gaily painted sign above the Bell and Bear, most realise that this pub has become one of the best places to pass a few hours as well as enjoying the many pub games on offer. The friendly banter of the sportsmen in the Bell and Bear seems very different from the leisure time pursuits of years gone by. But some connection can be found, if a few minutes are set aside to discover a little of Shelton's past.

In the Domesday Survey, Shelton was known as *Scelitone*. The word *Scelf* is Anglo-Saxon for 'shelf' and this describes the situation of the encampment on the ledge or shelf of the hill. It was far enough away from the wild animals to afford some protection with ample rough pasture for the livestock and arable land for strip cultivation. The disorganised huts around Snow Hill and Shelton Old Road soon became an organised village, with a manor house on the recently cleared land.

The township of Shelton which reached as far as Etruria and Queensway was, in 1200, the same as many other villages. But the life of the farmer, although ordered, was monotonous. Farm labourers enjoyed nothing better than a jug of rough ale while resting between the open fields around the land where, until recently, the speedway track stood. Leisure pursuits were simple: perhaps challenging each other on the accuracy of the throw of a knife against a target on one of the great oak trees, not unlike the dart throwers of today.

Gradually, farms that sold ale began to appear along the track to Hanley, places where travellers could rest and locals meet, all sharing each other's company.

Perhaps they used the clay found in the ground where the cemetery now stands, to roll into balls and skim along the ground at targets. As with today's sportsmen, wagers were commonplace. The lawn bowls of the gentry in the late 1500s, forever immortalised in the story of Sir Francis Drake at Plymouth, and the simple game of clay-ball rolling has changed, with the lawns becoming manicured green baize and the balls becoming a uniform shape and brightly coloured with a wooden stick to help the player sink the shot.

By late 1600s, Shelton Hall was one of the grandest buildings in the area. It was built mainly of local material, with stables for the horses and outbuildings for the livestock. The ancient and respected Fenton family lived there for many years and the hall was the birth place of the famous poet Elijah Fenton in 1683. When Charles and Ephraim Chatterley, eminent manufacturers, had the New Hall built in 1700, Shelton was altering fast..The grassy banks and thickets that covered the slopes were slowly changing into formal gardens with well laid out lawns and clipped hedges. By the time Joe Ridgway, a potter to H.M. The Queen, built his house on a site in Cauldon Place, Shelton was becoming quite a fashionable area to live.

All this building might have changed Shelton into just an extension of Hanley or Stoke if it were not for the fact that along with the grand houses small rows of terraced houses began to appear. First along Shelton Old Road, then gradually along the main road. The colliers and pottery workers who lived in these houses were considered rough by the upper classes, but they had built up a great camaraderie.

Rivalry existed between Shelton and neighbouring villages, and many local men frequented the ale house where the Bell and Bear now stands. In the 1700s, after gaining strength out of a pint mug, a group would often be egged on by the cheering crowd of regulars to make their way to the open ground around the Clough area to be met by equally lubricated men from other villages. The two champions would then slug it out until a winner was declared.

These bare-knuckled fights became quite an event with local champions praised wherever they went. Physical strength was idolised and the champion of the area would parade around, stripped to the waist and dragging his coat behind him. Treading on the coat was similar to throwing down the gauntlet and a fight would be arranged.

Tales were passed from one pub to another, often being exaggerated. One such tale was about fighter and inn-keeper Jack Cooper, who travelled miles to show off his prowess. When the great Irishman Don Donnelly heard of him, a fight was arranged. Unfortunately when Donnelly arrived in Shelton Cooper was out fighting in another part of the country. This so enraged Donnelly that he punched a hole through the inn door and told Mrs Cooper to tell her husband who had done it. Eventually Cooper was beaten by Donnelly in Ireland in 1815, although Cooper came home to a cheering crowd. A grim reminder of those fighting days is said to still exist in a pub in Ireland. Don Donnelly's strong right arm was preserved for prosperity in a glass jar on the bar. And, in the centre of Donnelly's Hollow, there is an obelisk commemorating the fight.

Cock-fighting, dog-fighting, bull- and bear-baiting were all popular sports enjoyed by working men in the late 1700s, with the upper classes growing richer from the wagers that took place.

Most of the workers who lived around Queen Anne Street area, where Signal Radio now stands, owned at least one terrier, bred especially for pitting against bulls and bears that were carted into the villages for the sole purpose of being set against the dogs. Here lie two good explanations of the pub's name. Possibly the area in front of the pub is where the animals' carts stood while the driver rested. The Bell part of the name may have derived from Bull. But, with local dialects and the passing of time the word may have been altered to Bell; or the name could refer to the bell that was rung to mark the beginning of the match.

The primitive bull ring was set up, probably not far from the pub. After the dog owners compared dogs and consumed a gill or two, the contest would begin. Although the horns of the bull were covered to protect the dog, the bull was still able to toss the animal high into the air; this practice, along with methods of egging either animal on, often ended in death.

Bear baiting involved the unfortunate animal being chained to a stake and there he would wait for the dogs to be set on him. Although he had the delicate parts of his anatomy protected, he was still open to the frightening attack of snarling dogs and yelling spectators, who, when they thought the pastime was not interesting enough applied blazing tar to the bear.

The railway came to the area in the 1800s with a grand station built on land known locally as Winton Wood, then still in the township of Shelton. Perhaps this brought a change to Shelton, or maybe it was the effect of John Wesley's visits in the mid-1800s who spoke with much affection of the area and its people. By the beginning of the 1900s, many of the gory sports had all but disappeared, though a few remained until recently. Distant relations of the less-violent sports are still talked about in the Bell and Bear. So next time you are travelling the road from Stoke to Hanley, call into the pub and look at the notice board to see the ways that Shelton people spend their spare time while enjoying the hospitality of the Bell and Bear.

SPRINGFIELDS

THE SPRINGFIELDS HOTEL

Although the area around the Springfields Hotel is not mentioned in the Domesday Book as a settlement, there were probably a few rough shelters in the clearing between the densely wooded areas beyond the settlements of Stoke and Penkhull. Gradually local people began to venture along the tracks made by the wild animals that drank from the Lyme Brook looking for new areas of land to cultivate.

The fires built for protection provided the heat needed for cooking. Coarsely ground grain and water provided the staple diet of these people. A form of bread was baked in the embers of the fires to sustain the people for many days while they were out in the Dark Wood towards The Spinney.

Passing travellers from the larger settlements would occasionally be given shelter on cold nights. Locals bartered the unleavened bread for a little yeast which gave the fresh bread a better texture and the baking tradition that was to become the cornerstone of Springfields had begun.

Trentham Priory Farm was said to have once stood on the land where the Springfields Hotel now stands, with its cloisters, stalls and arched doorways supplying a refuge to hungry and tired pilgrims on their way to Canterbury. Its fine barns occupied the site where the bakery now stands. The Grange stood at the junction of Clayton Lane.

The monks who lived within the Priory went about their daily tasks with a quiet serenity, tending the land, baking bread and probably brewing a sweet mead produced from the bees that swarmed around the many fruit trees in the area. The simple life of the monk was determined by his love and obedience for God. Centuries after the Priory had disappeared, the presence of one of these peaceful people was still said by many to be felt in the area around the hotel and bakery; perhaps his love and eagerness to work for God reached beyond his final resting place and he will forever tend to his chores peacefully oblivious of the passing of time.

By the mid-1500s, the fortification at Newcastle was falling into disrepair. The stones that once protected the Northern Earls from Hugh De Erdeswyck and Thomas De Swynneton were brought into the Springfield area to be used to build grand homes for the gentry. The Mansion

House that stood to the left of Clayton Lane until 1947 was built of these stones. A secret passage was said to have connected this building with Springfield House but its purpose is obscure.

Springfield House itself was very elegant in the 1800s, with lawns and a mounting block at the front and formal gardens to the rear. Many well-known families lived in the house over the years, each providing work for the local people, most of whom lived in cottages around Clayton Lane where the main settlement was beginning to grow. The staff of Springfield House was considered a little above the pot bank workers of Newcastle and the local tile manufacturer had began to use the clay in the ground. Affluent families like the Huntbachs gave the area by the brook an elegant appearance. Fine wines imported from abroad were laid out for the masters as they returned from their many trips to the textile towns of the north. Freshly baked bread was always on hand to share with the important travellers as they paused on their way to Newcastle. Even vagrants and Gypsies were looked after. Scraps from the tables were saved and given away at the back door to anyone who called for fear that some evil curse would be left.

The Great War brought drastic changes to the class system of the country house. Many able-bodied men took the King's Shilling and those that remained were insufficient to maintain the standard of living that the grand residences required. Land was sold and the gentry moved to smaller houses. When the soldiers came home new employment was needed and factories began to supply the growing needs of towns. After the Second World War the rural landscape had almost disappeared. This is where the modern Springfield Hotel came into its own, with ample space to suit all the needs of the modern traveller.

Most local people hold a few faded memories and a collection of black and white snaps taken with a Box Brownie; perhaps sitting outside the pub with the Austin Seven or Morris Minor, sharing a bottle of Ricki Orange, and trying to find the blue twist of salt in the crisps. This was a pleasant place to call on the way home from a visit to Trentham Gardens, with the aroma of the bakery drifting across the car park as the evening lights began to flicker along London Road.

Perhaps this is where this tale should end, before the juggernauts began to rattle glasses on the bar and coach trips to far-off places made Trentham Gardens less alluring. But the Springfields Hotel will always move with the times – even pub games and video entertainment now provide a lure for people as they pass by.

Most of these people only see one more pub, this one sandwiched between the Lyme Brook and the bakery with a facade that is somewhat out of place in today's high-tech architecture. Although there seems little call today for a staging post on the Newcastle to Stone Road the Springfield Hotel will provide, as it has done for many years, an oasis for visitors.

The Springfields

STOKE

THE WHEATSHEAF

It is hard to believe that the elongated facade with the gaudy posters of the Wheatsheaf Public House has seen anything other than groups of young people. People walking along Church Street nowadays only hear loud music and see the flashing lights of today's pub.

The Wheatsheaf is one of the oldest pubs in Stoke with the famous Red Lion succumbing to the planner's hammer in the 1960s. Only the figurehead and ornate balustrade were saved and even those have disappeared from Stoke to find a new home in the Crich Tramway Museum in Derbyshire.

Facing the busy bus stops, the Wheatsheaf stands as if to remind people of the great stage coaching days of Stoke. But even before those far-off days, Stoke was an important settlement. Although not occupied by as many people as its neighbours what made and will always make Stoke special is that it had and always will have a beautiful Parish Church.

There is evidence that religious rites of some form have taken place on the site of the present St Peters Church before 1066 AD. Although there was no township of Stoke until much later, it was the centre of a group of settlements and had the Mother Church of the parish. This consisted of Newcastle and Clayton to the west, Hanley and Norton in the Moors to the North and Lane End (Longton) to the east. Only a few fragments of that early history are still in existence but with a little time these can be unearthed.

Parts of a Celtic Cross dated at 100 AD were found near the site of the original Church; after spending many years as a support for the Priest Door in the Old Church and then lying by the vestry door in the new Church, these ancient remains were re-sited in the Church grounds to commemorate the Silver Jubilee of George V in 1935. The font inside dates from Norman times and its chequered history ranges from its use as a flower pot at Cliff Vale School (now St Dominic's), and then as a bird-bath in the church yard, until it was finally re-dedicated in 1932. The oak cover made in the 1600s originates from beams taken from the bell tower of St Peters in Wolverhampton.

Many great Potters found the open land around ideal at this time and Stoke began to earn its place in history. Dramatic changes were taking place and the landmarks of Stoke were beginning to form. A Town Hall was erected in Hill Street and the Coaching Inn, Church Street became a well-known landmark. The thrice-weekly coach, on its journey between Newcastle and Derby, called into the Wheatsheaf and the post coach called on its way to Newcastle which was, then, the postal centre of the area.

By the time the new Church was consecrated in the early 1800s Stoke had become quite a busy place. Drunkenness was commonplace as well as poverty and deprivation, for without any protection most of the working men and women were exploited by many master potters. Nevertheless some, like Wedgwood were socially enlightened to the fact that good working conditions made for healthier employees, which in turn meant more and better production.

Little thought was given to the heritage of the old Church and its stones when the building of the new Church began. It was left to Charles Lynam to have the arches that stand in the grounds constructed from the stones of the original church that he managed to salvage from Boothen Mill when it was demolished and the water course was filled in during the late 1800s. This was quite an achievement, as there were no plans of the original church for Lynam to consult.

The plaques and memorial tiles in the present Church have recorded forever the names of the people who gave a living to the people of Stoke-on-Trent. Josiah Wedgwood was born on the 12th July 1730 and died on the 3rd January 1795. He was interred in the Parish Church of Stoke, in the chancel of which a handsome mural monument by John Flaxman R.A. was erected to his memory. It reads:

"Who converted a rude and inconsiderable
Manufacture into an elegant Art and
An important part of National Commerce"

The tradition of pottery that began with Josiah Spode in 1760 still remains today and Minton connections with the Church and area are many-fold. Even the tiles that the congregation walk on today owe their existence to the Minton family.

By 1840 Charles R. Richardson who, according to Kelly's Directory was the licensee of the Wheatsheaf, was welcoming travellers from all over the country to his hostelry. With ample space for horses and good food, the hostelry flourished.

With the coming of the motor car Stoke began to alter, even the grand theatres first changing to picture palaces then cinemas replaced them, even these have disappeared. Only the Essoldo remains from the hey-day of film star worship. The only stars it sees now are those in the eyes of people when they call out a full line, in the never-ending games of Bingo played there.

What of the Wheatsheaf, perhaps a look of sadness appears on many faces when they pass on their way from the busier towns with its frontage now much smaller and offices and shops jostling for space. The Wheatsheaf still has a lot to offer people even today, the only difference is that instead of travellers with sturdy carpet bags containing fine clothes, many visitors today have instrument cases and leather jackets. Perhaps this typifies Stoke, a place that has to move with the times. Though other towns try to take its title away from it, Stoke will remain the centre of the city, always there but always open to the changing face and needs of its people.

Stoke Church: a tribute to Charles Lynam's building techniques

TALKE

THE QUEEN'S HEAD

To most people, Talke is just the end or the beginning of their journey, with the Queen's Head only a place to visit quickly. With one eye on the clock all of the time, most people can only half enjoy their drink and atmosphere of one of the oldest pubs in the area. Long before people's lives were governed by what time the next bus from Swan Bank leaves for Meir Square, or how long can they spend in the Queens Head until they have to head for home, Talke was a popular place.

Celtic man found the area between their settlement at Mow Cop and Audley ideal for habitation – with springs and pools to supply the water needed to sustain life and trees and rocks to build with. A settlement of primitive shelters began to appear on the clearing between the great wooded areas, these people probably gave the area its name, calling it "Talc" or "Tal" meaning high place.

By the 1200s, a scattering of low thatch-roofed cottages began to form into a village. The smoke and glow from their cooking fires made a guiding light for the hunters and travellers as they turned homeward from expeditions into the unfriendly and bleak land towards Church Lawton.

As with most communities, the landmarks that are the easiest to remember are the drinking places, with even a village as small as Talke having quite a few by 1600. Each had its own personality and catered for the needs of local people: public houses on the London to Manchester road, providing refreshment to travellers, to those that resemble houses with their front rooms. Of the few that remain, the Queens Head is one of the most popular.

One of the most remarkable stories concerns Joseph Fallows, whose life came abruptly to an end in 1781. He offered to steer a wagon carrying gun powder down the steep hill by the Ancient Cross while his friend, the original driver, refreshed himself in the Queens Head. Unfortunately, though led by two strong horses, the wagon went out of control. After colliding with houses on the roadside, it exploded into clouds of black smoke, killing Joseph and the horses, also causing a great deal of damage. The pub although shaken stood solid and hopefully will remain so for many years to come.

The Cross that they used for worship and meetings can still be seen at the top of the hill, having its base and foundation restored in 1887. The beautiful but tiny St Martins Church became an important landmark in the village when it was rebuilt in 1794. But, with an area as poor as Talke, improvements had to be added to the Church slowly as and when the public subscriptions allowed it. The superb stained glass window was not installed until 1888.

Methodism was gaining strength by the early 1800s. The Reverend Hugh Bourne's church, which he had built at his own expense in 1813, was patronised by enough people to warrant a bigger one being built on Coalpit Hill in 1876. The evils of drink were one of the main themes of the sermons at the chapel, and people looked at the regulars of the Queens Head with much disdain.

The timber-framed church of St Saviours was built shortly after the Primitive Methodist Church at the great cost of £4,000 to be sadly demolished in the 1970s. Of the other buildings that still serve as landmarks, one of the most memorable is the Toll House. This was built in the early 1800s, although all that remains of that angular building that

The Celtic cross – where Mr Fallows met his untimely end

was demolished in the 1920s is the small cross at the corner of Lindley Road and Congleton Road.

The area around Lindley Cottage once just part of rural landscape now seems somehow out of place. Bunkers Hill Colliery disappeared in the early 1900s but it, like its workers, are still remembered with much affection.

So just perhaps the rumbles that are often heard on warm summer's evenings are not just that of the traffic on the busy A500 heading to the M6 or trains bound for Crewe. They just might be that of poor Joseph's wagon coming down the Hill and, if strange happenings occur in the bar, perhaps it's the ghost of the original driver rushing to the rescue.

TRENTHAM

THE TRENTHAM HOTEL

The statue of a Roebuck (male deer) that greets people as they travel along Longton Road towards Trentham seems to baffle strangers. What connection does this traditional pub and restaurant have with an animal that has not roamed free in the area for many years? In fact, the Trentham Hotel was once called The Roebuck, for reasons which will soon be clear.

Trentham Hotel, or The Roebuck?

A settlement existed at Trentham long before the Romans invaded the land in approximately 200 AD. The relics that were excavated from a local burial mound show that people found the area suitable for habitation. While the ancient records of the first King of Mercia gave the location of Trentham as the site of one of the nunneries he formed in approximately 650 AD.

Anglo Saxon farmers at the time of the Domesday Book soon realised that the fertile land around the *ham* near to the river Trent was ideal for strip farming, and a small settlement with groups of cottages began to appear. A simple Church was built and a community was born. The tracks first made by animals began to form into primitive roads between this settlement and the growing settlements of Wolstanton and Blurton.

The animals that once roamed free were now killed for their meat and for sport, great herds of deer would be hunted in The Kings Wood that was in sight of the land where the Trentham Hotel now stands, so intense was the hunting that by the Middle Ages the numbers had decreased dramatically

Even now it is not difficult to understand why, when the Duke of Sutherland purchased great portions of land, he chose an area between the old road to Barlaston and Whitmore to build his home.

The gentry and their family believed that all intelligent people lived like them in grand houses, with elegant rooms, formal gardens, sumptuous food and fine wine. But many visitors to the area came from more modest origins. This road to Trentham was popular with people looking for a better life in the country away from the deprivation and dirt and was always quite busy with townspeople.

Although the facts of the following story, as with many tales told at Grandma's knee, perhaps there is more than a little truth in it.

After watching her family succumb to one of the many cholera outbreaks in the mid-1800s, Ada left her window-less home in Spatglade with her few possessions and began the long walk to Penkhull and the Stoke-on-Trent parish work house.

After many days and nights sleeping in animal shelters, first in the Penfold farm area, then on the Heath, she took shelter at the edge of the Trentham estate. The ale house proved very welcoming even to a child eight years of age. Ada was able to earn her keep by helping with odd jobs for the licensee whose name, according to Kelly's Directory of 1840, was Charlotte Swift.

Some time later the butler from the hall, while visiting the pub, made enquiries about employing Ada as a scullery maid. Ada packed her things, thanked the licensee and went to the hall.

As time passed, her duties included helping the kitchen staff to prepare for a grand celebration. After spending many hours scrubbing vegetables Ada was getting tired but there was still lots to do. It was decided that a special jam tart was to be the dessert, followed by a light sponge cake. Ada's task now was to add the jam to the tarts and beat the sponge. Absent-mindedly, she added the sponge to the tarts. After chastising her, the cook realised it was too late to make a replacement dessert and carried on.

After the cake was cooked decorations were added and the meal was served. Ada listened at the door for a reaction before packing her bags again, but the response from upstairs was favourable and she kept her job but not the credit for the meal. The cook made her swear to secrecy, with a threat of instant dismissal if she revealed the secret. For many years people came from miles around to try to discover the recipe that was known only to Ada and the cook.

By 1911, Trentham Hall was sold and much of the great estate was used for leisure time activities. Ada ended her days telling those she considered close friends how she invented one of the most popular dishes in the area, The "Trentham Tart".

Perhaps the heyday of the area was the 1950s, when most people enjoyed nothing better than a glorious day out. Perhaps a picnic and short trip on the miniature railway pulled by tiny locomotives with romantic names like Golspie and Dunrobin through the woods at Trentham Gardens to the outdoor swimming pool fed by natural springs. Rarely a weekend went by in the summer without true love being found on a boat or by the summer house at Trentham Gardens. The grand ballroom saw the coming of the modern dances with Reg Bassett's band always giving some style to the evening.

Like the area in which it stands the Trentham Hotel will probably undergo even more changes before the next century. The road to Trentham is becoming less of a special place where plans for a better future can be made. One thing is certain though Trentham Hotel will always remain special.

TUNSTALL

THE PARADISE INN

Most people think they have to wait until their maker calls before they can see paradise. But all they have to do is to take a short walk along Wesley Street, Tunstall. To outsiders, Tunstall may seem just another of the five towns that Arnold Bennett wrote about with such eloquence in the 1900s. But Tunstall was beginning to be quite a busy town by the time John Wesley visited the area in the late 1700s. Perhaps, like him, since the time the first travellers saw the area between Endon and Nantwich people have chosen to live here because it is one of the most pleasant of places around.

The Paradise Inn

Anglo Saxons decided to build a small group of dwellings, where the Newcastle to Biddulph track crossed the Cheadle to Nantwich Road. This small town or *Tun* along with the outbuilding or Stalls for the animals gave the inhabitants reason to proudly call the area *Tun-Stall*.

The Fitzwarine, Audley, Bowyer, Sneyd, Greasley and Badderlys are just some of the family names that gradually changed the tiny hamlet into a thriving town.

Before John Wesley came on horseback from Birmingham only a minority of the working class people of Tunstall had any choice regarding religion. A few devoted families went regularly to church, while most of the people preferred to find a little peace from the everyday life in the ale houses.

The market places and open fields around Tunstall were the best places for Wesley to preach, giving him a chance to talk to the ordinary working people and giving them a hope for a better future, away from the evils of strong drink and loose living. Gradually people were converted into Wesley's form of Methodism.

Tunstall blacksmith Joseph Capper was converted in the early 1800s, but when the Chartist meetings began to be held in Tunstall, Joseph would stand by his anvil in Market Place and declare to the assembled crowd the hypocrisy of the factory owners and clergy. They were, he said, "Gaining great riches out of the neglected poor." At the age of 65 Joseph was sentenced to prison for Sedition. On his return to Tunstall after two years' imprisonment in Stafford Gaol he was broken in both spirit and health and died just a few years later.

Another of the sons of Tunstall was Charles Shaw whose book "When I Was a Child" gives quite a vivid insight into the squalid life of pottery families in the mid-1800s.

The area where the Paradise public house stood was considered quite elite, with Charles Davenport the surgeon living there in the late 1800s.

Religion was gaining strength all the time and by the time Louisa Wain held prayer meetings in her home Hoster House in the late 1800s there was a call for a mission. This was to become the Church of St. Chads at Chatterley for which she laid the foundation stone.

Small shops and houses stood alongside the flourishing business and factories in the mid-1800s, with Absolom Wood designing quite a few of the new buildings at that time. The Methodist Church, Town Hall, Free Library, Science and Art School and Fire Station all bear his individual marks. Gradually a Public Library and Museum grew. These and many other buildings gave the town its formal shape, with Woods enthusiasm for Art Nouveau most evident in a small shop in Paradise Street.

Although the air of Tunstall was filled with the smoke from coal burning fires, and the noise from clogs against the cobbles echoed along the High Street, the town was an ideal place for artistic talent to grow. One of the most famous daughters of the town was born on a cold January day in 1899 to Harry and Ann Cliff. Clarice's younger life was occupied with simple schooling at the Elementary and Summerbank Schools, after which she became an apprentice enameller where her artistic talent was noticed. She then went on to become well known not only for bold designs on pottery but also her style which was so typical of the twenties. Her work is much valued now as perfect examples of Art Deco.

Perhaps many people will think Tunstall will just fade into the sea of houses that began to appear after the Second World War. Like the Paradise Inn, Tunstall has had to undergo major refurbishment to move with the times, with only the most solid of its foundations left intact.

Maybe this is the case, but with so many notable people having their roots firmly embedded in the clay around the centre of Tunstall, those who can claim a link with Tunstall will know a little bit of home they call heaven is not far from the Paradise Inn.

The Library and College

UBBERLEY

THE MAN O' CLAY

Perhaps the best way to describe The Man o' Clay public house is a tastefully decorated pub on a modern housing estate with all the facilities needed by people both young and old who frequent the carefully decorated rooms. A health centre, schools and a library help to make the area between the B5040 and the A52 quite an independent community, with something for everyone. But there was a time when the land was just open fields with few scattered dwellings.

Bentilee: pink shrimps in the water?

The old people had their work, with days filled with so much hard toil that there was hardly time for a night out. Younger people now have access to the Health Centre, children attend the schools on the estate, and everbody can use the library, before joining that never-ending stream of people who use the Man o' Clay as a meeting place. Perhaps listening to the stories of someone who spent their childhood within the area now known as Bentilee will give those who are slightly curious an insight. Like this one:

Rene was born in 1909 one of a family of nine and, although her family were not able to give her some of the finer things that the children from the bigger houses had, what she did have was the beautiful countryside to play in. Young Rene would play happily in the fields where the old Ubberley hall once stood, skipping over the stones that once made the birth place of the Verdons of Alton. The spring rain would make the ground around what is now Beverley Drive alive with flowers to pick. If she was very quiet, she just might see the sparrow hawk as it began to make its nest in the long grass by Rookery farm. Early summer would mean long walks to Willots Wood where great drifts of bluebells could be gathered eagerly. Rene believed the tales told by the older children that the first bluebells appeared to mark the spot were some poor soldier of long ago met his sad demise, the colour and the way they grew in drifts were just his blue blood spilled so gallantly for his King and Country.

One of Rene's favourite games was trying to catch the yellow frogs that lived in the streams that criss-crossed the area. Only occasionally did she manage to take one home in the pocket of her dress.

The water that most of the people used had to be collected from the well. Although cool and clear, the water often contained small shrimps; this would give much amusement to the small children as they carried the water in buckets along Ford Hayes Lane.

High summer brought its own pleasures with more than one game played. Rene was told of buried treasure left by the Roundheads at the time of the Civil War. Golden Rod would mark the spot where the treasure lay. Many days were spent with the older children digging around the area where the Man o' Clay pub now stands – perhaps the next plant would by the right one. Although she had a vivid imagination, she only half believed this and the other stories, such as foxgloves being used for the fairies as mittens.

Bilberries were picked by groups of children and sold in bowls to anyone with a few coppers to spare; this and the fresh watercress that grew in abundance gave Rene just a few pennies to spend at the shops in Dividy Road. Another way of earning money was to run errands for the older people in neighbouring cottages, one such message led to a hangover for two of Rene's family. Sally and George were sent out one hot summer's evening to fetch a jug of strong ale from the Wagon and Horses public house, the expedition went well until they reached Ubberley Road on the way back. George, the younger of the two, suggested just a little sip to moisten his dry lips, then Sally became tired and thirsty; gradually the walk became slower and the jug less full. On fear of punishment, the children decided to have another sip before topping the jug up from one of the many tributaries of the brook. When they arrived home, they left the beer for their father and retired to the outhouse to sleep off the effects. Only when their father saw the fresh water-shrimps in the dregs of the jug did he realise something was amiss. The hangover felt by the children when they were woken up was by far much worse than any punishment meted out by their father.

This ideal life changed suddenly when at thirteen most children including Rene went to work. Rene was chosen to work at Widow Field farm at Hulme. The farm was owned by the Brassingtons, a family of some importance. One permanent reminder of their contribution to the area is the Jubilee Well which bears the name Thomas Bettany Brassington.

Life was hard, with Miss Lancaster as her employer Rene's day began at 6.30 am. With few friends of her own age she began to class the livestock as her friends. Dolly, their pony, would look forward to seeing Rene as she carried the fresh straw and oats. As part of her work she loaded the cart with churns prior to delivery. The measures that hung around them made a friendly clatter as the cart made its way through the lanes of Ubberley. Milk was sold at the cottage gates; a gill, half gill and quarter gill of fresh milk was sold for the sum of a penny, a half penny and a farthing.

The next family Rene worked for was the Sidalls, here her service was as housemaid and she was paid the grand total of three shillings a week. This fortune allowed Rene to take money home to help keep the family. Time off from service at the Sidalls gave Rene a chance to help with household chores.

The most laborious of this was wash day, which began early Monday morning. Her task was to light the boiler that stood in the corner of the scullery, the wind that blew under the door across the quarry floor caused the flame to go out as she tried to get the fire going. Hudson soap was then added, turning the clear water a milky colour while the water heated. It was Rene's job as the eldest to sort out the washing while Sally dollied the heavily soiled work clothes of her father in the dolly tub. With the three-legged wooden stick and galvanised pozzie, the whites were then boiled and Elsie's job was mixing the blue bag solution ready for the final rinse in the brown slop sink. After this, the hard labour of the mangling began.

By now Rene's poor reddened arms ached with the heavy work of retrieving clothes from the depths of that hot tub with only a stick softened with years of hot water to help. George would turn the handle of the two-wheeled instrument of torture, which without concentration would chew short sleeves and split the buttons. Sally caught and folded the still damp clothes in a basket. While Rene produced even more sheets which went through the rollers at least twice to ensure less ironing.

Even on a cold winter's day the lines that stretched from the house to the privvy were filled with frozen stiff washing. Rain altered the process and the clothes horse was spread-eagled round the roaring fire and indoor lines were covered with clothes. The whole house would be filled with a warm smell that Rene remembered long after the dolly tub was to be replaced by a washer purchased from the money Rene and the rest of the family saved.

As Rene grew, so did the houses on the road from Hanley to Weston Coyney. By the 1960s, nothing was left of the fields were she played; the cottages were to be replaced by smart houses with indoor toilets and hot water. No more lighting the boiler, no more running to the public house for a gill of ale for father. Beer was sold neatly packaged in take-home packs and public houses are places to take the family for a night out. Nevertheless, nothing will ever replace a great meeting place and there are few better in the area than the Man o' Clay.

WERRINGTON

THE WINDMILL

When visitors call into the Windmill to take refreshments, how many stop to think about the travellers who paused here long ago? This short history will try to find out.

Salt was conveyed on a Roman Road in 200 AD, which ran through Werrington – not, as you might think, following the present road, but diagonally from Chester, cutting along Salters Lane to Green Lane Roughcote, Caverswall, Forsbrook and beyond to Rocester. Many a weary traveller must have paused for refreshment on the sheltered ground before taking that long journey into the wooded area of Caverswall.

By 400 AD, fierce immigrants travelled the coast line of Britain looking for inlets; the Trent was just one of their highways, and when the river became un-navigable they abandoned their primitive craft and pushed inland until they found a suitable settlement area. On chief by the name of Werringa made his settlement beyond "Bucca's Secret Place" (Bucknall) near the forest valley, watered by a stream and sheltered by two hills. *Werringas-Ton* was born.

The settlements of the De-Werynton Family were probably in the vicinity of the present Church School and Library. By the 13th century, it had gradually widened, with small dwellings scattered on the hillside giving shelter to the travellers who passed by. The Subsidy Roll of 1427 gives a guide to parishioners who were wealthy enough to pay property tax. Unfortunately, there is no reference to the De-Werynton family, and this might be because the direct line had come to an end – but Werrington carried on.

The early 16th century brought boundary wars, with Werrington having ill-defined lines and turf cutting on Wetley Moor as an important part of the local economy. By the 17th century, mining and iron-works began to break the rural landscape at Werrington with probably the primitive Windmill to grind corn and making a good resting place for the peasant labourers. The mid-1700s saw Werrington with its first stone windmill and a turnpike road to alter the way of life again. The miller's house made a good staging post for the travellers who passed from Bucknall on their way to Cheadle.

In Whites Directory of 1851, a Mr Greatbach was the miller as well as innkeeper. The pace of life changed quickly from then on, with the School and Detention Centre being built in 1870. William Forister was the miller in 1880, when he took over the public house and began the long line of publicans who gave the Windmill its reputation as one of the most popular hostelries in the area.

The Windmill, Werrington, 1906

WESTON COYNEY

THE WESTON COYNEY ARMS

Most public houses look striking when the sun shines on them or when they are alight with coloured and fluorescent lights. But the Weston Coyney Arms with its heraldic sign swinging outside seems to have the wonderful ability of showing its true colours any time. Having the appearance of a manor house of long ago, set in front of a small wood, the exterior is only outshone by an interior decor with interesting fireplaces and wood panelling.

Although this public house was built in the 20th century, it stands on approximately the same site of one of the famous toll-gate houses that helped to keep the roads of Staffordshire in good repair in the mid-1700s. This road joined Longton to Leek for many years. For without any waterlogged low ground, it was easier to travel on. The area now covered by the postal code of Weston Coyney has been, since time began, an important part of community life.

When the great warrior chiefs began to divide the area into separate settlements, some grew at a faster rate than others with the prosperity of the settlements depending greatly on the ferocity of its leaders. Although the leader of the settlement to the west of Caverswall was not as fierce as his neighbour, he kept his warriors in order with the sword and a fighting ability that was known for miles around.

Gradually the small settlement at Weston (Coyney) grew and by the time of the Domesday Survey quite a few simple dwellings were beginning to appear along the main tracks. With good arable land and fresh water streams as well as wetland meadows for cattle the area could produce most of the food it needed.

By 1600 the uniform shape of Weston was forming, with the great timber-framed Park Hall standing at the edge of what is now a Country Park. A few moated farmhouses remained from the time when some form of protection was needed against the marauding Celts facing Caverswall and the River Blythe. Although much of the area was quite prosperous, many people still lived in small thatched cottages earning their living in any way they could. Farming was still the most important occupation, but a few of the young people were gaining employment in other ways. All of the dwelling places of these people have gone now as well as the great houses. Only a few stones remain where the great home of the Parker family once stood. Park Hall was, even by today's standards, important. It was surrounded by dense woodlands, alive with foxes and birds which the gentry would hunt, mainly for sport. While it is said that the beautiful village hall now stands on the foundations of what was Weston Coyney Hall, slightly smaller than Park Hall but still making a good home for the Coyney family. Only a name is left to remind people where one of the last moated farm houses once stood. To most people that is all that is left of the rich heritage of Weston Coyney. Nevertheless, a few people seem able to give an explanation of more than the visual signs of yester-year and to a side of Weston Coyney that is not publicised when a formal history is compiled.

Perhaps this is one of the tales best told by some of the great story tellers that still live in Weston Coyney. It is best told on a winter's nights at the Weston Coyney Arms but hopefully this version will uncover some unexplained phenomena in the area around the Weston Coyney Arms.

Daisy lived with her family in a small cottage at the edge of Birch Wood which, in the 1600s, covered most of the area now occupied by the houses of Defoe Drive. When her mother died in one of the many smallpox outbreaks Daisy was left in charge of the family, quite a task for a girl of 13. Her life was a constant routine of cooking and cleaning, which she did willingly, always managing to sing as she walked through the woods collecting eggs from the few wild chickens that laid their eggs under the holly bushes for protection.

When one of the men employed at Park Hall took a shine to her, Daisy blossomed and began spending what little free time she had meeting Charlie in Birch Wood and Weston Sprink where the bluebells and wild daffodils flowered in the spring. As their love and the summer grew, Daisy and Charlie decided to set up home on a small plot of land. This faced the main Leek Road, between Bolton Gate Farm and one of the few remaining moated houses with the fast-lowing River Blythe running close by and plenty of land for farming.

Suddenly the idyllic dream was shattered when the Civil War came to the area. Charlie fought hard against the Puritan soldiers when they found him drinking home brewed ale not far from his master's house. As one of the cannons rumbled over his crumpled body, he struck a fatal blow to a soldier and his shouts were only for Daisy. On hearing his dying cries from her fathers house where she had taken refuge Daisy ran along the rock hard track in the wood. With the help of a farm cart and the determination of love she carried Charlie's broken body to his family home at the crossings of Weston Coyney Road and Weston Road to hide him. With the help of his family she buried her beloved Charlie there with no marker in case the soldiers returned. She then walked to the home that she and Charlie had such great plans for. Her body was found two days later. Although many said her death was from exposure her family knew that Daisy died of a broken heart.

Parkhall Lake: little visible evidence of Charlie's last fight

It is still said today that some echoes of that fateful day can be heard in Weston Coyney and, until recent years, the lake where Charlie's body was first broken often ran dry as the ghost of a Puritan soldier looked for the killer of his comrade. The cottage at the crossroads was replaced first with a toll-house and then an inn, then in recent years a modern pub named "Lautrec's" in honour of the artist. The ghost of Charlie can still be felt as he crawls on his knees trying to help Daisy to hide him.

While Daisy's sad spirit can occasionally be heard by regulars of the public house near the River Blythe where she died.

Only Weston Sprink, Birch Wood and the Weston Coyney Arms echo with the sounds of Daisy's laughter and the sweet sounds of voices as she and Charlie enjoy each others company.

Perhaps cynics would reject this story, but like most histories that are passed down by word of mouth truth is often stranger than fiction. Only the very hard hearted could not be touched by this story of undying love.

Next time the wind rattles the doors and windows of the Weston Coyney Arms and visitors ask for the heating to be turned up a little higher, maybe that whispering in the corner is just a young couple trying to plan a future that can never be.

The Weston Coyney of today is growing fast with houses of all shapes and sizes scattered about on ground that until the 1960s was described as farming and mining land, bur don't think that's where Weston Coyney ends. While there are people living in the area, there will always be tales to tell.

FAVOURITE RECIPES:
from the snugs and bars on a sunday lunch time

ADA'S TRENTHAM TART

8oz (225gm) short crust pastry
4 tablespoons of self raising flour
2 tablespoons of sugar
2oz (50gm) of margarine
milk to mix
3 tablespoons of raspberry jam.

Method: Line a tart tin with the pastry then spread the jam. Cream the margarine and sugar together until it looks like cream adding the milk to mix. Spread the mixture on the jam-covered base. Bake at Regulo/Mark 7 (220^{0}C/425^{0}F) for about 25 to 30 minutes to cool and decorate with glaze icing and cherries.

OLD OSWALD'S OATCAKES

Method: Mix fine oatmeal with water until a thin batter is achieved. Add a pinch of salt, then pour a small ladle full onto a hot griddle; turn with a palate knife when set.

Serve warm with bacon and cheese for breakfast or, better still, call into one of the many oatcake shops on the way to work and purchase some expertly-cooked ones.

LARRY LOBBY

1lb (450gm) of scrag end of beef, cut up
2 pints (1 l) of cold water
1 strip of celery cut up; 1 large carrot diced
1 small turnip diced
1 onion chopped
1lb (450gm) potatoes diced
2 tablespoons of pearl barley
1 teaspoon of salt
stock cube

Method: Bring the meat to the boil and remove any scum, add diced vegetables, barley and seasoning. Simmer for at least 2 hours and serve with fresh crusty bread.

BAZZERS "CHICKEN" PIE

8oz (225gm) puff pastry
2 plump pigeons freshly drawn
8oz (225gm) lean gammon
15 fl oz (400ml) chicken stock
small bunch of herbs
salt to taste
3 carrots
1 tablespoon of dripping

Method: Cut each pigeon in half along the breast bone. Dice the gammon and slice the carrots. Turn lightly in dripping for 15 minutes, drain from the fat and arrange in a large pie dish with herbs. Cover with puff pastry. Brush with beaten egg and bake at Regulo/Mark 8 (2300ºC/450ºF) for 15 minutes. Reduce heat and continue to cook for a further 40 minutes. Heat stock and pour into the pie crust, serve hot with mashed potatoes, vegetables and thick gravy.

TRIGGER'S JUGGED HARE

1 hare
A pint and a half of stock
juice of small lemon
2 tablespoons of dripping
1 tablespoon butter
1 tablespoon plain flour
1 onion
bunch herbs
salt and pepper

Method: Cut the hare into joints, then cut up the pieces with a saw. Fry in the dripping until brown, then place into a deep casserole dish. Add the onion, herbs, lemon juice, salt and pepper and stock.

Cover dish and cook on Regulo/Mark 3 (170ºC/325ºF) for 3 hours.

Mix the flour and butter together, stir into the stock and return to the oven. Pile pieces onto a very hot dish and strain the gravy over. Serve with red currant jelly.

BERTHA'S BEST BREWED TEA

2 tablespoons of best loose tea.
Half a pint of fresh milk.
6 pints freshly boiled water.
Sugar to taste.

Method: Warm the Brown Betty. Add the tea to which the boiling water must be added immediately . Stir and allow to brew for 5 minutes, then add the milk to the pot. Will make at least 12 good cups.

ERIC'S ELDERFLOWER 'CHAMPAGNE'

7-8 Heads of Elderflowers (picked on a dry day away from the road)
2 tablespoons of white vinegar.
$1^1/_2$ lbs sugar
1 gallon of cold water.

Method: Put the elderflowers, vinegar, lemon juice and sugar into a large crock or plastic fermenting pail. Pour on the cold water, leave for 24 hours. Strain though muslin or a fine meshed sieve. Put into screw-topped bottles, screwing the tops on lightly at first and then gradually tightening them over the next few days. After 14 days the 'champagne' is ready to drink. Readers may be familiar with the 1993 court case which disputed the right of a small English purveyor of soft drinks to use the phrase 'Elderflower Champagne'; at the time of writing, an appeal was pending!

Index

We publish a wide range of titles, including general interest publications, guides to individual towns, and books for outdoor activities centred on walking and cycling in the great outdoors throughout England and Wales. This is a recent selection:

General interest:

THE INCREDIBLY BIASED BEER GUIDE – Ruth Herman
This is the most comprehensive guide to Britain's smaller breweries and the pubs where you can sample their products. Produced with the collaboration of the Small Independent Brewers' Association and including a half-price subscription to The Beer Lovers' Club. £6.95

DIAL 999 – EMERGENCY SERVICES IN ACTION – John Creighton
Re-live the excitement as fire engines rush to disasters. See dramatic rescues on land and sea. Read how the professionals keep a clear head and swing into action. £9.95

THE ALABAMA AFFAIR – David Hollett
This is an account of Britain's rôle in the American Civil War. Read how Merseyside dockyards supplied ships for the Confederate navy, thereby supporting the slave trade. The *Alabama* was the most famous of the 'Laird Rams', and was chased half way across the world before being sunk ignominiously. £9.95

PEAK DISTRICT DIARY – Roger Redfern
An evocative book, celebrating the glorious countryside of the Peak District. The book is based on Roger's popular column in *The Guardian* newspaper and is profusely illustrated with stunning photographs. £6.95

I REMAIN, YOUR SON JACK – J. C. Morten (edited by Sheila Morten)
A collection of almost 200 letters, as featured on BBC TV, telling the moving story of a young soldier in the First World War. Profusely illustrated with contemporary photographs. £8.95

FORGOTTEN DIVISIONS – John Fox
A unique account of the 1914 – 18 War, drawing on the experience of soldiers and civilians, from a Lancashire town and a Rhineland village. The book is well illustrated and contains many unique photographs. £9.95

ROAD SENSE – Doug Holland
A book for drivers with some experience, preparing them for an advanced driving test. The book introduces a recommended system of car control, based on that developed by the Police Driving School. Doug Holland is a highly qualified driving instructor, working with RoSPA. £5.95

Books of Walks:

There are many books for outdoor people in our catalogue, including:

RAMBLES IN NORTH WALES
– Roger Redfern

HERITAGE WALKS IN THE PEAK DISTRICT
– Clive Price

EAST CHESHIRE WALKS
– Graham Beech

WEST CHESHIRE WALKS
– Jen Darling

WEST PENNINE WALKS
– Mike Cresswell

STAFFORDSHIRE WALKS
– Les Lumsdon

NEWARK AND SHERWOOD RAMBLES
– Malcolm McKenzie

NORTH NOTTINGHAMSHIRE RAMBLES
– MAlcolm McKenzie

RAMBLES AROUND NOTTINGHAM & DERBY
– Keith Taylor

RAMBLES AROUND MANCHESTER
– Mike Cresswell

WESTERN LAKELAND RAMBLES
– Gordon Brown

WELSH WALKS:
Dolgellau and the Cambrian Coast
– Laurence Main and Morag Perrott

WELSH WALKS:
Aberystwyth and District
– Laurence Main and Morag Perrott

MOSTLY DOWNHILL:
Leisurely walks in the Lake District
– Alan Pears

WEST PENNINE WALKS
– Mike Cresswell

– all of the above books are currently £6.95 each

CHALLENGING WALKS IN NORTH-WEST BRITAIN
– Ron Astley *(£9.95)*

WALKING PEAKLAND TRACKWAYS
– Mike Cresswell *(£7.95)*

Long-distance walks:

For long-distance walks enthusiasts, we have several books including:

THE GREATER MANCHESTER BOUNDARY WALK
– Graham Phythian

THE THIRLMERE WAY
– Tim Cappelli

THE FURNESS TRAIL
– Tim Cappelli

THE MARCHES WAY
– Les Lumsdon

THE TWO ROSES WAY
– Peter Billington, Eric Slater,
Bill Greenwood and Clive Edwards

THE RED ROSE WALK
– Tom Schofield

FROM WHARFEDALE TO WESTMORLAND:
Historical walks through the Yorkshire Dales
– Aline Watson

THE WEST YORKSHIRE WAY
– Nicholas Parrott

– all £6.95 each

The Best Pub Walks!

Sigma publish the widest range of "Pub Walks" guides, covering just about every popular walking destination in England and Wales. Each book includes 25 – 30 interesting walks and varied suitable for individuals or family groups. *The walks are based on "Real Ale" inns of character and are all accessible by public transport.*

Areas covered include

Cheshire • Dartmoor • Exmoor • Isle of Wight • Yorkshire Dales • Peak District • Lake District • Cotswolds • Mendips • Cornwall • Lancashire • Oxfordshire • Snowdonia • Devon

… and dozens more – all £6.95 each!